EXCEPTIONAL TREES
of LOS ANGELES

by
DONALD R. HODEL

Text and Photos
by

DONALD R. HODEL

Environmental Horticulture Advisor
University of California
Cooperative Extension

Published by the
CALIFORNIA ARBORETUM FOUNDATION, INC.
Sponsor of the Los Angeles State and County Arboretum

Produced by:
  Catered Graphics, Chatsworth, CA
    Executive Editor: Richard M. Ray
    Art Director: Russ Heinze
    Copy Editor: Alvin Horton
    Production Editor: Kathleen S. Parker
    Book Production: Janine M. Hunter
    Typography: Linda Hernandez
    Map Production: Steve R. Hunter

Color by:
  Colorscan Systems, San Diego, CA
    Executive Coordinator: Carol Jones
    Production Manager: Sandra Clark
    Color Supervisor: Ross Ferrelet

Maps provided by:
  Perry Supply Co., Inc./MAPS, etc., Canoga Park, CA

Printing and Book Manufacturing by:
  Lake Book Manufacturing, Inc., Melrose Park, IL
    President: Ralph Genovese
    Production Coordinator: Susan Cascarano

ISBN 0-9621121-0-0

Library of Congress
Catalog Card Number: 88-7548

CONTENTS

ACKNOWLEDGMENTS

My indebtedness and gratitude to the members of the Exceptional Trees of Los Angeles Committee are beyond words. The quality and magnitude of their contributions are highly evident on the following pages.

Exceptional Trees of Los Angeles Committee

Mary N. Asher, Landscape Designer, Sherman Oaks
Samuel Ayres, Jr. (deceased), La Canada
Mario Baltazar, Tree Trimmer & District Supervisor, Road Department, County of Los Angeles
James A. Bauml, Taxonomist, Los Angeles State and County Arboretum, Arcadia
Robert N. Berlin, Landscape Consultant, South Pasadena
David M. Brown, Conservation Chairman, Santa Monica Mountains Chapter, California Native Plant Society, Calabasas
Mel Camarillo, Valley Crest Tree Company, Sepulveda
Riley Caudill, Arboriculturist, City of Pasadena
Philip E. Chandler, Landscape Designer, Santa Monica
Francis Ching, Director, Department of Arboreta and Botanic Gardens, County of Los Angeles
James L. Degen, Professor of Ornamental Horticulture, California State Polytechnic University, Pomona
John Delgadillo, Tree Trimmer & District Supervisor, Road Department, County of Los Angeles
Ken Dyer, Superintendent of Parks, City of Redondo Beach
Jon Earl, Tree People, Beverly Hills
Thomas W. Escherich, Street Tree Inventory Coordinator, City of Los Angeles
Morgan "Bill" Evans, Landscape Architect, Malibu
Michael E. Hall, Educator, Southern California Regional Occupational Center, Torrance
Grace Heintz, Santa Monica

Frances W. Hotchkiss, Landscape Designer, Santa Monica
Robert W. Kennedy, Superintendent, Los Angeles Street Tree Division, City of Los Angeles
Norman Krueger, District Tree Supervisor, Road Department, County of Los Angeles
Peter K. Lang, Los Angeles
Norma Le Valley, South Pasadena
Andy Lipkis, Director, Tree People, Beverly Hills
Marcelino G. Lomeli, Park Superintendent, City of Beverly Hills
Mildred E. Mathias, Emeritus Professor of Botany, University of California, Los Angeles
Robert L. Meyer, Park & Golf Course Superintendent, City of Cerritos
David Mings, Assistant Roadside Trees Superintendent, Road Department, County of Los Angeles
Ray E. Montgomery, Landscape Architect, City of Pasadena
Kathy Musial, Botanist, Henry E. Huntington Library, Art Gallery & Botanical Gardens, San Marino
Roy Ontiveros, Turfgrass & Landscape Consultant, Kellogg Supply, Inc., Pomona
Raymond E. Page, Landscape Architect, Beverly Hills
C.J. Pilkerton, Line Clearing Forester, Southern California Edison Company, Rosemead
John Provine, Superintendent, Los Angeles State and County Arboretum, Arcadia
Herbert A. Spitzer, Jr., Deputy Forester, Department of Forester & Fire Warden, County of Los Angeles
Douglas Stafford, Park Superintendent, City of Santa Monica
Don Stockard, Branch Manager, Valley Crest Tree Company, Sepulveda
Don Torres, Street Tree Superintendent, City of Cerritos
Robert D. Traut, Lecturer, Department of Ornamental Horticulture, California State Polytechnic University, Pomona
David S. Verity, Senior Museum Scientist, Mildred E. Mathias Botanical Garden, University of California, Los Angeles
Neil S. Weikel, Landscape Architect, Santa Monica

Many others have contributed in various ways to this book and deserve recognition. I express my gratitude especially to the following who have contributed information about trees and various historic sites: Helen Treend, the "Oak-Tree Lady" of Chatsworth; Don Walker, Horticulturist, Torrance; Ellen Calomiris, Curator, Rancho Los Cerritos, Long Beach; Pamela Seager, Director, Rancho Los Alamitos, Long Beach; Elizabeth McClintock, Research Associate, Botany Department, University of California, Berkeley; Earl Wood, Curator, Shadow Ranch, Canoga Park; Barry Herlihy, Executive Director, The Cultural Heritage Foundation of Southern California, Heritage Square, Los Angeles; Beverly Nairne, Reference Librarian, San Marino Public Library; Tim Snider, Horticulturist, Pasadena; Carol Crilly, Curator, Workman & Temple Homestead, Industry; Glenn Hiatt, Director, Leonis Adobe Association, Calabasas; Jean Bruce Poole, Senior Curator, and Teena Stern, Researcher/Archivist, El Pueblo de Los Angeles State Historic Park; William Heideman, Executive Director, Hollenbeck Home, Los Angeles; Zoe Bergquist, Director, Banning Residence Museum, Wilmington; Hanne Mielke, Arcadia; Kathleen Kelly, Dean, Kimiko Morita, Librarian, and Sister Mary Irene Flanagan, Mount St. Mary's College, Los Angeles; Al Peiler, Landscape Horticulturist, Hotel Bel-Air, Bel-Air; Christie Phillips, Associated Historical Societies of Los Angeles; Joe Da Rold, Executive Director, Whittier Historical Society; Elva Meline, Curator, San Fernando Valley Historical Society, Mission Hills; Robert Tatsch, La Casa de Carrion, San Dimas; Ginger Elliott, Executive Director, Claremont Heritage, Claremont; Steven Daugherty, Horticulturist, Sunland; Kevin Johnson, Landscape Horticulturist, Pomona; Steve Orloff, Agronomist, University of California Cooperative Extension, Lancaster; Bill McKinley, Assistant Park Planner, City of Glendale; John Bleck, Biology Department, University of California, Santa Barbara; Richard Palmer, Whittier; Bill Newbro, Public Relations, Automobile Club of Southern California, Los Angeles; Ralph Bassett, Landscape Supervisor, and Scott Saunders, Landscape Technician, Rancho Los Amigos Hospital, Downey; Michele Guffanti, Docent, and Debbie Schafer, Dan Martin, and Pam Raffeto, Curators, Los Encinos State Historic Park, Encino; Pat Winston, Virginia Robinson Gardens, Beverly Hills; M. B. Preeman, Brentwood; Mike Hathaway and Tim Lorman, Los Angeles Country Club; George Caldwell, Santa Monica; Francis Burroughs, Docent, Manuel Dominguez Home, Rancho San Pedro, Compton; Craig Castillo, Pasadena; Elliane Welch, Los Angeles Cultural Heritage Commission; Katsumi Kunitsuga, Executive Secretary, Japanese-American Cultural & Community Center, Los Angeles; Rich Hawkins, Jeff Spector, Bill Woodland, Steve Bear, Stephanie Carey, and Glenn Johnson, United States Forest Service, Angeles National Forest; Kay Hartman, American Forestry Association; Margaret Mauk, Claremont; Kevin Long, Palomares Adobe, Pomona; Thomas Brown, Landscape Architect, Berkeley; and Farrell Dickman, Grounds Supervisor, Fred C. Nelles State School, Whittier.

A special thanks must go to Joan DeFato, Librarian, Los Angeles State and County Arboretum, who went to extraordinary efforts to track down innumerable references containing background material on the trees included here in addition to reviewing the manuscript.

Research was partially supported by a grant from the University of California, Division of Agriculture & Natural Resources, Elvenia J. Slosson Endowment Fund for Ornamental Horticulture. In addition, the County of Los Angeles partially supported travel within the County during this time. I am deeply grateful to these institutions for their support.

My appreciation is also expressed to Nicelma J. King, County Director, University of California, Cooperative Extension, for her unwavering support; George D. Rendell, Acting County Director, for his encouragement and interest; and the various staff members with whom I share a common office for their interest, support, and the pleasure of working with them.

Bringing this work to its appropriate fruition would not have been possible without the generous and selfless contributions of Richard M. Ray, President, Horticultural Associates, who guided the development of this book through its seemingly endless phases of production. Mr. Ray's extraordinary ability to take a manuscript and transform it into a visually pleasing and tasteful book is self evident on these pages.

I extend my heartfelt thanks to Paul Weissich, Director, Honolulu Botanic Gardens, Hawaii, for contributing valuable information about a similar project in Hawaii and with whom I share a unique interest in trees.

I would be remiss if I did not express my gratitude to my father, Robert J. Hodel, whose expert instruction in photography enabled me to take the colorful photos accompanying this book and who unknowingly fostered my interest and appreciation of trees and other plants.

Lastly, I thank my wife, Marianne, and children, Robert and Christina, for their encouragement and patience while accompanying me for many long hours in the field and who tolerated my preoccupations and foibles with grace and understanding.

Donald R. Hodel
Los Angeles, California
August, 1988

PREFACE

Exceptional Trees of Los Angeles is a product of the Los Angeles County office of the University of California Cooperative Extension. Cooperative Extension is the public service and information program operated by the University of California in 55 counties throughout the state. In Los Angeles our program offerings are quite varied: Environmental Horticulture (of which this book is a product); Consumer Marketing; Home Economics and Nutrition; 4-H Youth Development; Agronomy; and Resource Development. Our programs are made available to the people of Los Angeles County at no charge.

This volume was originally an applied research project developed and excuted by our office's Environmental Horticulture Advisor, Donald R. Hodel. As a professional trained in horticulture and a concerned environmentalist, he wanted to document for the people of Los Angeles County some of the most unusual and beautiful trees of our area in the hope that they can be preserved for our posterity. He received an enabling grant from the Elvenia J. Slosson Endowment Fund administered by the Division of Agriculture and Natural Resources of the University of California. We are proud to have his excellent work published by the California Arboretum Foundation.

Dr. Nicelma J. King
County Director
University of California,
    Cooperative Extension
Los Angeles

CALIFORNIA ARBORETUM FOUNDATION, INC.
In Celebration of Its 40th Anniversary

The California Arboretum Foundation and the County of Los Angeles Department of Arboreta and Botanic Gardens have worked hand in hand to develop one of the most outstanding plant collections in the world. Dr. Samuel Ayres, who thought there should be more color in the Southern California landscape, was originally inspired with the idea of creating an arboretum that would make possible the introduction of flowering plants to our area. The California

Arboretum Foundation was established in 1948 to make this dream a reality and the founding Trustees' eight original goals continue today as the mission of the Los Angeles State and County Arboretum:

1. A horticultural center for Southern California
2. A center for the introduction, testing and improvement of plants adaptable to Southern California
3. A gardening school for professionals and amateurs
4. A center of research and scientific study
5. A horticultural library and herbarium
6. A publication center for information of horticultural, botanical and historical interest
7. A preserve of buildings and gardens
8. A bird sanctuary

Goal Six has had particularly popular applications. The Arboretum has sometimes been called "the garden of knowledge" — a place of publishing, teaching and learning. It was in this spirit that the current Board of Trustees listened with interest and approved the publishing proposal for this book. The proposal was presented by Francis Ching, Director of the Department of Arboreta and Botanic Gardens, and also a member of the Exceptional Trees of Los Angeles Committee. The California Arboretum Foundation is proud, that through its funding, this special book could be nurtured to its final printed form. It will be showcased at the 8th Annual Los Angeles Garden Show at the Arboretum, October 14-23, 1988.

The Foundation is the non-profit funding organization that supports the Arboretum and finances educational projects such as this important book. We pay tribute to the thousands of Foundation members and friends whose time, energy and gifts have assisted the Arboretum over the years. Our special gratitude goes to those sponsors listed separately on page seven and to the Men's Garden Club of Los Angeles.

We are proud that many of the exceptional trees selected by the Committee are located on the Arboretum grounds. They have been viewed by millions of visitors over the years.

Finally, our compliments for an outstanding horticultural achievement to the author, Donald R. Hodel, the Exceptional Trees of Los Angeles Committee and the Los Angeles County offices of the University of California Cooperative Extension. Just as these trees add so much to our heritage, so will this book.

Alice Frost Thomas, President C.A.F.

Richard A. Grant, Jr., Vice President and Chairman, Development Committee C.A.F.

Richard M. Ray, Chairman, Publication Committee

Francis Ching, Director Department of Arboreta and Botanic Gardens County of Los Angeles

SPONSORS

The following sponsors have generously contributed to the production of this book:

Scott Laugharn Adair	William G. King, III
David R. Arnold	Hoyt B. Leisure
Richard M. Baker	O. E. McCartney
Olin Barrett	Lowry B. McCaslin
David N. Barry III	Albert B. McKee, Jr.
Wilbur Bassett	Dr. Clark D. McQuay
Edward M. Benson, Jr.	Robert P. Miller, Jr.
Thomas L. Brennan	George F. Moody
Robert J. Brookes	J. Stanley Mullin
George A. Brumder	Peter W. Mullin
Ernest A. Bryant III	Bob R. Offenhauser
Campbell and Campbell	Arthur L. Park
William M. Carpenter	Mr. & Mrs. Richard M. Ray
Robert W. Cheesewright	Joseph Ryan
Mr. & Mrs. Francis Ching	Alexander Saunderson
Michael Conner Corley	Fred Schoellkopf
Erwin H. Craig	Walter R. Schoenfeld
David M. Davis	Constance M. Shanahan
William T. Drysdale	James A. Shanahan
Daniel L. Duggan	William W. Smith, M.D.
George W. Elkins	Mrs. Christina Spies
Peter L. Fitzpatrick	Savas Jerry Stathatos
Don Freeberg	Carl H. Tasche
George N. Gibbs, Jr.	Waller Taylor, II
Teresa Gonzales	L. Sherman Telleen
Richard A. Grant, Jr.	Lois E. Tepas
Ed N. Harrison	Mr. Starr Teriitahi
Fred L. Hartley	Alice Frost Thomas
Robert Carey Hill	William M. Tomlinson
Hazel M. Hodel	Robert Van Dine
Robert J. Hodel	Robert J. Van Dyke
Saburo Ishihara	L. J. Whitney, Jr.
Paul G. Johansing	Robert E. Wycoff

FOREWORD

Los Angeles County is fortunate in its horticultural heritage beginning with the many introductions of plants by the Franciscan fathers and augmented in the golden days of the large estates whose gardens contained plants from all parts of the world. In more recent decades with the development of public arboreta and botanical gardens, plant introductions are continuing. The Los Angeles area is doubly fortunate that unlike many parts of the world it contains a variety of soils, in a set of diverse climates with a myriad of microclimates, making it possible to grow plants native to temperate as well as tropical regions. This book is the first record of some of the unusual trees that have survived in Los Angeles County in spite of continuing urbanization.

It is interesting to look at their countries of origin, by far the largest number of them being from Australia. Included also are trees from Africa, Asia Minor, Southeast Asia, Europe, South America, China, Japan, Mexico, India, and the U.S. including 14 that are native to California.

Ernest H. Wilson, the great plant explorer, in *Aristocrats of the Garden,* recognized the uniqueness of California:

In California the trees and shrubs of the temperate regions of the Southern Hemisphere thrive amazingly, and it is probable that in this state alone a greater variety of woody plants can be successfully grown in the open ground than in any similar area in the world. I mention the Southern hemisphere, but it should be added that the trees and shrubs of China, Japan, the Himalayas, Southern Europe, the Caucasus, and the Mediterranean region of Northern Africa are equally at home in California.

This book is confirmation of that statement, and giving recognition to some of the exceptional trees in Los Angeles County will increase our appreciation of this rich heritage and protect it for the pleasure of future residents.

Dr. Mildred E. Mathias
Professor Emeritus of Botany
University of California
Los Angeles

INTRODUCTION

The variety of trees cultivated in the various municipalities and unincorporated areas of Los Angeles County — nearly 1000 species — is perhaps unmatched by any other area of similar size in the world. This fact is due in part to the county's long and colorful history of horticulture dating back to the days of the Spanish missions in the 18th Century. Also, its diverse climatic zones from desert and alpine areas inland to frost-free, nearly tropical areas near the coast make it possible to grow trees somewhere within its boundaries from almost any region of the world. The county's wealth of tree species includes a few exceptional specimens that stand out above all others of their kind. Unfortunately, continual urbanization and renovation and redevelopment of existing urban areas have destroyed or jeopardized many of them.

This book is the result of a study aimed at locating and documenting exceptional trees so that their status could be publicized to heighten public awareness of their value as community assets worthy of protection and preservation.

Entitled the Exceptional Trees of Los Angeles (ETLA), the study began in 1984. In September of that year, a committee composed of distinguished horticulturists and botanists was formed to assist the author in identifying candidate trees to be considered for designation as exceptional. A pool of more than 1000 trees resulted from this effort, and the author spent nearly 800 hours and drove 5000 miles from late 1984 through 1986 to photograph these candidate trees and collect information about them. To be considered as exceptional for this study, a candidate consisting of either a single tree or group planting of the same kind of tree growing within Los Angeles County was evaluated according to these criteria: age, historical or cultural value, esthetic quality, endemic status, location, rarity, and/or size including height, girth of the trunk at chest height, and spread of the branches.

There are 167 trees from various municipalities or unincorporated areas in the county that were selected and designated as exceptional. These trees comprise 125 species in 80 genera representing 36 families of flowering plants (angiosperms) and cone-bearing plants (gymnosperms).

The trees are presented alphabetically by their botanical or scientific names, followed by their common names. The names of each tree are followed by a letter and number code. Each letter corresponds to one of the seven geographical regions of the county, each of the seven shown on a map at the back of the book. Each number corresponds to a number on the map of that geographical region, denoting the location of the tree. For example, below is the exceptional *Acer macrophyllum* or California big-leaf maple followed by the code **SFV 10.** This means that this particular tree is number 10 in the geographical listing and on the map for the San Fernando Valley region. The geographical listing and the map numbered with the location of each tree will facilitate locating the tree and making arrangements to view it (see pages 71-78). Some of the trees are on private property; please be respectful of the owners and always request permission to enter private property.

Acer macrophyllum.   SFV 10
CALIFORNIA BIG-LEAF MAPLE.
(Not Pictured)

Acer, the Latin name for maple trees, also means sharp, referring to that capacity of the wood that enabled Romans to use it for spears. A native of Oregon and California, this maple with attractive, deeply lobed leaves is one of the finest hardwoods in the West, yielding high quality lumber prized for use in furniture, flooring, and boats. It was highly esteemed by Indians, who made canoe paddles from its fine wood.

Only about a dozen stands of California big-leaf maple remain in the Santa Monica Mountains. The group located on Cold Creek off Stunt Road near Calabasas is the densest and contains the largest specimens.

Acrocarpus fraxinifolius.   SE 1
PINK CEDAR.

Acrocarpus combines the Greek words *akros,* meaning top, and *karpos,* meaning fruit, referring to the fruit being held high at the top of the tree. Native to the monsoon forests of Burma and India, this deciduous to nearly evergreen tree is not a cedar but a member of the bean family.

Uncommon in the landscape, these four extraordinary specimens support a profusion of scarlet flowers arranged in dense clusters on bare branches in early to late spring. This exceptional planting is located on the north side of the 1100 Building on Erickson Avenue at Rancho Los Amigos Hospital in Downey. Founded in 1887 as a work farm for Los Angeles County's infirm indigents, the County Poor Farm, as it then was known, has since been renamed Rancho Los Amigos and today houses county facilities and rehabilitation programs for the physically handicapped.

The pink cedar is noted for its profusion of scarlet flowers in dense clusters in early to late spring.

This Queensland kauri is the tallest of its kind in the continental United States.

Agathis robusta.   C 9
QUEENSLAND KAURI.

Agathis is a group of cone-bearing trees native from Malaysia to the Philippines, Australia, New Zealand, and the southwestern Pacific, where it can attain an immense size. *Agathis,* Greek for a ball of thread, refers in this case to the appearance of the catkins or reproductive structures of the female kauri trees. The trees are a source of a gum called dammar or copal, used in the manufacture of some varnishes.

Located in Elysian Park, only a mile from downtown Los Angeles, this kauri is 93 years old and more than 97 feet tall, making it the largest of its kind in the continental United States. Rare in the landscape, this imposing tree is a remnant of Southern California's first botanic garden, Chavez Ravine Arboretum, established in 1893 by the Los Angeles Horticultural Society for the purpose of introducing new trees to Los Angeles. Several of the original trees of this garden, representing the oldest and largest of their kind in California, are still standing in the area west of Stadium Way between Scott Avenue and Elysian Park Drive.

A striking parkway planting, gum myrtle is noted for its smooth trunk with bark peeling to reveal cream, rose, and mauve.

Angophora costata. PSM 2

GUM MYRTLE.

Angophora, about 8 species of trees native to eastern Australia, is named from the Greek words *agnos,* meaning jar or vessel, and *phoreo,* meaning bearing, referring to the trees' cup-like fruits. A close relative of *Eucalyptus,* gum myrtle is noted for its striking, smooth trunk with bark peeling to reveal irregular patches of cream, rose, and mauve. In Australia, aboriginals used the bark and leaves to produce dyes. Gum myrtle is rare in the Los Angeles landscape. This striking parkway planting of 20 large trees is located in the 1500 block of Kenilworth Avenue in Pasadena.

PASADENA PSM 1
(Not Pictured)

This exceptional planting of four handsome gum myrtle trees is at the entrance to the Annandale Country Club in Pasadena. One tree, more than 45 feet tall with a spread of 60 feet and a trunk nearly 12 feet around, is the largest of its kind in California.

Leaves of the bunya-bunya are flat, leathery, sharply pointed, overlapping, arranged in a spiral fashion.

Araucaria bidwillii. SE 2

BUNYA-BUNYA.

Araucaria is a group of about 18 species of cone-bearing trees native only to the Southern Hemisphere, from New Guinea to Australia, New Caledonia, New Zealand, and Chile in South America. The name is derived from Arauco Province in southern Chile. Evidence of their lengthy existence has been found in fossils 60 million years old. Located at Rancho Los Amigos Hospital in Downey, this notable specimen is more than 90 feet tall.

The bunya-bunya, native to the forests of Queensland in Australia, is a unique and peculiar conifer with glossy dark green, flat, leathery, sharply pointed, overlapping leaves arranged in a spiral fashion along the branches. The fruit of the bunya-bunya is a cone, the shape and size of a pineapple and weighing up to 10 pounds. It becomes a lethal object when falling from a tree. The large, flat seeds, called bunya nuts, require three years to mature in the cone and are an important source of food for aboriginals as well as wallabies.

This hoop pine was planted in the 1880s in San Dimas.

Araucaria cunninghamii.   SGV 22
HOOP PINE.

Hoop pine is native to Australia and New Guinea, where it becomes a large tree in mountain forests and is logged extensively for its wood. This remarkable specimen, located at the historic San Dimas Mansion in San Dimas, is the oldest and largest of its kind in California. It was planted in the 1880s and today is more than 100 feet tall.

Designed as a hotel by Joseph C. Newsom, one of California's best known architects in the 1880s and constructed in 1887 by the San Jose Land Company during Southern California's first land boom, the San Dimas Mansion has never had a paying guest. Before it was completed and could be occupied, the real estate market collapsed and the hotel was sold and changed hands several times. It was finally bought and used as a residence in 1889 by J. W. Walker, a pioneer citrus grower, who was instrumental in developing San Dimas into one of the first centers of the citrus industry in Southern California. The hotel, with its distinctive sunburst decorations, ornamental cupola, balconies, and long veranda, is a classic example of Victorian Era architecture in California.

An impressive planting of star pines is at the Veteran's Administration Hospital in Brentwood.

Araucaria heterophylla.   W 19
STAR PINE, NORFOLK ISLAND PINE.

Native to Norfolk Island, a 19th Century British penal colony east of Australia, the star pine is a distinctive and formal tree characterized by its pyramidal shape and uniform layers of whorled branches appearing as spokes on a horizontally set wheel. Whorls of young branches at the top are star shaped, hence the common name. This extraordinary planting, situated in an expansive lawn area at the Veteran's Administration Hospital in the Brentwood area of Los Angeles, contains the largest specimens in Southern California.

The Norfolk Island pine is the best known of the araucarias in North America. It is grown extensively in California, Florida, and Hawaii as a potted decorative plant for indoor use or as an exterior landscape plant in mild regions.

Archontophoenix cunninghamiana.
KING PALM.

Archontophoenix is named from the Greek words
archontos, meaning chief or majestic, and *phoenix,*
meaning palm. This grove of king palms comprising
several hundred individuals is the largest planting of
this species outside its native Australia.

Planted in 1915, the grove is located in the Virginia
Robinson Gardens at one of the first homes to be built
in Beverly Hills. Virginia Robinson, the last owner
and heir to the Robinson's Department Store fortune,
willed her estate to the County of Los Angeles, Department of Arboreta and Botanic Gardens, upon her
death in 1977. This dense grove is much as one would
find it in its native rain forest habitat with naturalized
seedlings and offspring of all ages and sizes intermin-
gled with the parent trees.

King palms at the Virginia Robinson Gardens form a dense grove.

Well suited to
residential yards,
baphia has a
spreading, multi-
trunked habit, glossy
dark green leaves,
showy white flowers.

Baphia chrysophylla.
BAPHIA.

Baphia, a group of about 70 species of trees and
shrubs in Africa and Madagascar, is named from the
Greek word *baphe,* a red dye extracted from the wood
of some species. This small, handsome, spreading
multi-trunked tree with glossy dark green leaves and
clusters of showy white flowers appearing in an axil-
lary fashion along the ends of the branches in early
summer is the only one of its kind in the United States.
Located in Elysian Park in Los Angeles, it is a remnant
of the old Chavez Ravine Arboretum. Well suited to
residential yards because of its smallness and handsome flowers and foliage, *Baphia* is worthy of much
wider cultivation.

Bauhinia variegata. SE 16
ORCHID TREE.

Spectacular in late spring or early summer, the orchid tree is covered profusely with pink, lavender, purple flowers.

Bauhinia, a group of more than 250 species of trees, shrubs, and vines native to warm regions of the globe, is named in honor of two brothers, Johann and Caspar Bauhin, illustrious Swiss botanists of the 16th Century. Although a member of the bean family, the orchid tree was given its common name because of its flowers, which bear a superficial resemblance to an orchid.

Situated as a street planting in the 13400-13700 block of Walnut Street in Whittier, these trees are a spectacular sight in late spring to early summer, when the bare branches are covered profusely with the light pink, lavender, and orchid-purple flowers.

Largest of its kind in California, this toog in Whittier has fibrous, reddish-brown bark.

Bischofia javanica. SE 7
TOOG.

Bischofia is named in honor of Gottlieb Wilhelm Bischoff, professor of botany at Heidelberg University in Germany in the early 1800s. Native from Indonesia and Malaysia to Polynesia, the toog is highly esteemed for its useful wood and medicinal properties. It is said that in Malaysia tigers clean their claws by scratching the bark of the toog. Very few specimens of this tropical tree are cultivated in California. Growing at a private residence on Rideout Way in Whittier, this is the largest of its kind in California, with a trunk 5 feet around and more than 65 feet tall.

13

Brachychiton acerifolius.

FLAME BOTTLE TREE.

Brachychiton is named from the Greek words *brachys,* meaning short, and *chiton,* meaning a tunic, referring to the short hairs covering the fruit and seed. The tree can be spectacular in early summer, when it wholly or partially drops its deeply lobed, maple like leaves to reveal great clusters of pink to red, bell-shaped flowers.

This flame bottle tree, native to Australia and one of the first of its kind introduced to California, is more than 45 feet tall, spreads 55 feet, and has a trunk 9 feet around. It was planted in the 1890s by Andrew McNally, famous Chicago atlas publisher who introduced many plants, trees, and birds from around the world onto his 2,000 acre Windemere Ranch in present-day La Mirada. The tree stands adjacent to the original McNally ranch home, named the Neff Mansion after McNally's son-in-law and first ranch manager, Edwin Neff. The Neff Mansion and surrounding grounds are now part of Neff Park in La Mirada.

McNally was a pioneer rancher in southeast Los Angeles County who made significant contributions to Southern California agriculture. More than 700 acres of his ranch were devoted to olives and citrus, making La Mirada an important source of olive oil in the early 1900s. In fact, at its peak, more olive oil was shipped throughout the United States from McNally's ranch than from all of Italy.

In early summer the flame bottle tree can have great clusters of pink to red, bell-shaped flowers.

Pink flowers of the white kurrajong are often followed by interesting, fuzzy, golden-brown, persistent pods.

Brachychiton discolor.

QUEENSLAND LACEBARK, WHITE KURRAJONG.

Kurrajong is derived from the Australian aboriginal word *currajong,* meaning fiber-yielding plant. With its leafless branches supporting terminal clusters of pink, fuzzy, cup-shaped flowers, the Queensland lacebark is a spectacular sight in early summer. This exceptionally large specimen, more than 45 feet tall and with a trunk almost 9 feet around, is located at the corner of 8th Street and Dartmouth Avenue at the Claremont Colleges, a group of six affiliated colleges established in 1888 in Claremont. At the peak of its flowering, the ground beneath the tree is a carpet of pink flowers.

Flowers are followed by interesting, fuzzy, golden-brown, persistent pods which split longitudinally to reveal clusters of rounded seeds. Like all brachychitons, the Queensland lacebark is native to Australia and seems to flower most profusely following a dry spring.

Brachychiton populneus. C 11

BOTTLE TREE, BLACK KURRAJONG.

Bark fibers of the black kurrajong are used by Australian aboriginals to make nets, fishing lines, and dilly bags. Also, they use the roots and seeds for food, the latter eaten raw or roasted or made into a coffee-like drink. Although large, with a spread of more than 55 feet and a trunk nearly 15 feet around, this remarkable tree is atypical of its kind. Its multi-trunked habit is quite different from the single trunk more typical of this species, broad at the base and tapering sharply to the first branches so to appear bottle-shaped. Located in Elysian Park in Los Angeles, this specimen is a remnant of the old Chavez Ravine Arboretum and is the oldest of its kind in California.

This atypical, multi-trunked black kurrajong in Elysian Park has pendulous, white, bell-shaped flowers and persistent black pods. Like all brachychitons, it is drought tolerant once established.

A street planting of Guadalupe palms such as this at the Huntington Botanical Gardens achieves a formal and elegant effect.

Brahea edulis. PSM 8

GUADALUPE PALM.

Brahea is a group of fan palms native to Mexico and northern Central America. The name honors the noted 16th Century Dutch astronomer, Tycho Brahe. Native to Guadalupe Island off the western coast of Baja California, this particular species has fruits containing an edible but fibrous pulp, hence the name *edulis*. This *grande allée* planting at the Huntington Botanical Gardens in San Marino is the largest mass grouping of this formal and elegant palm outside its native habitat.

These palms were some of the earliest plantings of rancher, financier, art and book collector, and plant lover Henry E. Huntington on his estate in San Marino in the early 1900s. Today the Huntington Library, Art Gallery, and Botanical Gardens house world-famous collections of books, art, and ornamental plants in formal and informal gardens attracting more than 500,000 visitors and hundreds of researchers and scholars each year.

An old and large cape chestnut flowers profusely in Elysian Park.

This cape chestnut in Arcadia has an outstanding dome-shaped crown, curious fruits.

Calodendrum capense.   C 12
CAPE CHESTNUT.

Calodendrum is named from the Greek words *kalos,* meaning beautiful, and *dendron,* meaning a tree. Native from the Cape Region of South Africa north into tropical regions and a member of the orange family, the Cape chestnut is one of the choicest flowering trees for the Los Angeles area. This extraordinarily large specimen, a remnant of the old Chavez Ravine Arboretum in Elysian Park in Los Angeles, spreads nearly 80 feet, has a trunk 10 feet around, and was the first introduced to California.

Although the tree is evergreen, leaves can be completely hidden by the profuse display of white-to-pink-to-lilac flowers in terminal spikes that blankets the tree in early summer. Flowers are followed by a grayish, woody pod that splits open in a flower-like fashion to reveal shiny, black angular seeds. The seeds were once thought by Xhosa hunters in South Africa to have magic properties and were attached to their wrists while hunting to increase skill and luck. The best known cape chestnut in Africa is in Kenya at the Tree Tops Hotel, where branches from this tree grow through the building.

ARCADIA   SGV 19

Although not quite as large or old as the specimen in Elysian Park, this Cape chestnut tree at the corner of Floral and Santa Anita Avenues in Arcadia is exceptional due to its almost perfect, dome-shaped crown and exquisite and profuse flower display in early summer.

Carya illinoensis.   SFV 3
PECAN.

The pecan is a graceful and stately tree native to the southern and central United States. *Carya* is named from the Greek word for walnut tree, *karya,* and the pecan is a not-too-distant relative of this well known nut. In Greek mythology, Carya was also the name of the daughter of the King of Laconia who was changed into a walnut tree by Bacchus. This magnificent planting, lining the east side of Balboa Boulevard in the Sepulveda Dam Recreation area near Reseda in the San Fernando Valley section of Los Angeles, contains many large, stately specimens.

Large, stately pecans line Balboa Boulevard near Sepulveda Dam.

The white sapote is prized for its delicious, sweet fruit variously described as similar in flavor to a peach or banana.

Casimiroa edulis. SE 3

WHITE SAPOTE, MEXICAN APPLE.

The white sapote, native to the mountains of Mexico and Central Mexico, was introduced to California in the early 1800s by the Franciscan missionaries. The name *Casimiroa* honors Cardinal Casimiro Gomez de Ortega, 18th-century Spanish churchman and botanist. The word *edulis* refers to the edible, yellow, tennis-ball-sized fruit variously described as similar in flavor to a bland peach, sweet banana, or a banana-peach custard. The species sports attractive, palmately compound, glossy, dark green leaves. This large and exceptional specimen is located on Erickson Avenue at Rancho Los Amigos Hospital in Downey.

The bark, leaves, and seeds contain a glycoside (casimirosine) used medicinally by the Aztecs and modern-day Mexicans to calm rheumatic pains, cure diarrhea and ulcers, and induce sleep. A small dose produces deep sleep lasting for several hours. In Nahuatl, the Aztec language, it was called *cochiztzapotl,* meaning sleepy zapote.

Castanospermum australe. PSM 9

MORETON BAY CHESTNUT, BLACK BEAN.

Castanospermum is named from the Greek words *castanea,* meaning chestnut tree, and *spermum,* meaning seed, referring to the resemblance of the seeds to chestnuts. It is uncommon in the landscape. This striking specimen is adjacent to the Art Gallery at the Huntington Botanical Gardens in San Marino.

A member of the bean family, the Moreton Bay chestnut is noted for its attractive, evergreen, shiny, dark green, compound leaves which grow up to a foot in length and its stiff spikes of bright red and yellow flowers produced directly on older branches and sometimes even on the trunk. Brownish, bean-like pods up to 8 inches in length and containing several chestnut-like seeds follow the flowers and hang directly from the woody branches. In its native Australia, aboriginals roast and eat the seeds, which are poisonous if eaten raw. Cattle have died from eating large quantities of seeds. The wood of the Moreton Bay chestnut finishes like teak and is one of the most highly prized and valuable cabinet woods in the world. Prior to the development of synthetic insulators, it was used extensively in electrical switchboards due to its high resistance to current.

The Moreton Bay chestnut has attractive, dark green, compound leaves, stiff spikes of red and yellow flowers, bean-like pods.

HORSETAIL TREE, IRONWOOD, RIVER SHE-OAK.

Casuarina, a group of 40 to 50 peculiar and interesting species of Australian trees and shrubs, derives its name from the Latin *casuarius,* referring to the resemblance of its twigs to the feathers of the cassowary bird. The wood is extremely hard and similar but inferior to true oak. This explains the common names ironwood and she-oak, the 'she' being the Australian Bushmen's term indicating something of inferior quality. This notable parkway planting covers a one-mile stretch of Lindbrook Drive between Hilgard and Devon Avenues near UCLA in the Westwood area of Los Angeles. Among the nearly 200 trees are many large and well-shaped specimens distinctive in their silhouette and texture.

The horsetail tree bears a strong resemblance to the pines because of its small woody, cone-like fruits and thin, jointed, rod-like twigs, 3-7 inches long and 1/16 inch in diameter. These pendulous, pine-needle-like twigs resembling a horse's tail are green and function as leaves. However, unlike the pines, it is a flowering plant whose true leaves, scale-like and only about 1/64 inch long, and tiny, petalless flowers are virtually invisible.

Tolerant of a variety of adverse environmental conditions including wind, salinity, heat, and wet or dry soils, the horsetail tree has been planted extensively for windbreaks, reforestation, and bank and soil erosion control throughout the warmer regions of the globe. It has naturalized in many areas.

Over 200 ironwood trees with pine-needle-like leaves and cone-like fruits line Lindbrook Drive in Westwood.

Largest in California, this Chinese cedar in Elysian Park has woody, star-shaped fruit capsules that look like dried flowers.

CHINESE CEDAR, BURMESE CEDAR.

Cedrela, a group of trees native to the Himalayan region of Tropical Asia from India to China, is named from the Latin word for cedar, *cedrus,* to which the Chinese cedar is similar in fragrance and appearance of the wood. Actually, the Chinese cedar, or *toon,* as it is called in India, is a close relative of mahogany and is often substituted for it. This specimen, a remnant of the old Chavez Ravine Arboretum in Elysian Park in Los Angeles, is the largest of its kind in California.

The wood of the *toon* is highly esteemed for cabinet work and is resistant to rot and insects. This rare, handsome, deciduous tree is noted for its attractive new foliage tinted in various shades of pink and red and long pendulous clusters of white flowers in late spring and early summer. The flowers have a honey-like fragrance and, in India, are a source of a saffron-yellow dye used during the Bosant festival. The flowers are followed by woody, star-shaped, dehiscent capsules that look like dried, preserved flowers.

Cedrus atlantica 'Glauca'. PSM 10

BLUE ATLAS CEDAR.

Cedrus, a group of about five species native from northwest Africa to the Himalayas, is named from the Greek word *kedros,* referring to a resinous tree. This particular species is native to the Atlas Mountains in Morocco. Located on the grounds of the Huntington Botanical Gardens in San Marino, this splendid specimen is noted for its striking silvery-blue color and has been given the cultivar name 'Glauca'. It is the original specimen of this particular cultivar and, being vegetatively propagated, all blue Atlas cedars now in the landscape are genetically identical descendants of this tree.

All blue Atlas cedars in the landscape are genetically identical descendants of this tree, noted for its silvery-blue color.

This deodar cedar at the San Dimas Mansion is over 100 years old, largest in the area.

Cedrus deodara. SGV 23

DEODAR CEDAR.

Although a native of the Himalaya Mountains, these stately majestic trees are right at home in the Los Angeles area. This particular specimen, situated next to the historic San Dimas Mansion in San Dimas, is 100 years old, a mere 94 feet tall, and has a trunk 12 feet around.

SAN DIMAS SGV 24
(Not Pictured)

Located near the intersection of Iglesia Street and Bonita Avenue in San Dimas, is another large deodar cedar. It was planted in 1900 by Robert M. Teague, a leading citrus nurseryman at the turn of the century, at what then was his ranch home.

ALTADENA PSM 3

This famous double planting of deodar cedar trees, the first of their kind in the United States, is on that portion of Santa Rosa Avenue, known as Christmas Tree Lane, between Woodbury Road and Las Flores Drive in Altadena. The trees were planted in 1882 along what then was the driveway to the home of John Woodbury, a rancher and land developer.

About 170 trees line mile-long Christmas Tree Lane, and, although beautiful at any time of year, they are most spectacular during the last two weeks of December, when more than 10,000 colored lights strung through the trees are illuminated to honor the Christmas season. They were first lighted in 1920 and have been dark for only two Decembers since then, once during World War II and again in 1973 during the energy crisis.

About 170 deodar cedars line Christmas Tree Lane in Altadena.

This cedar-of-Lebanon was brought from the Holy Land in 1888.

Cedrus libani. SE 10

CEDAR-OF-LEBANON.

Civilizations throughout Biblical times extolled the virtues of this tree. It was the royal tree, the "lion" of trees, and the glory of Lebanon. The tree symbolized grandeur, might, majesty, dignity, and lofty stature. It was so highly prized that one invader of Lebanon, Semnacherib, in 700 B.C., boasted that he would come to Lebanon and destroy all the cedars. No greater blow could be dealt to the people of Lebanon by an enemy. This outstanding specimen, located in the 11200 block of E. Howard Street in Whittier, survived several months in shipment from its native Holy Land and was planted in 1888 by Mrs. Harriet Strong on what then was the Strong Ranch. The tree is now more than 60 feet tall with a trunk nearly 13 feet around.

Much referred to throughout the Bible, the cedar-of-Lebanon was highly esteemed and preferred above all others for its vigor, beauty, age, and fragrance and durability of the wood. It repels insects and was used by the Egyptians to encase their mummies. When Solomon was faced with the task of completing the great temple begun by David, he sent 30,000 Israelites, 150,000 slaves, and more than 3,000 officers to cut and harvest the tremendous stands of cedar trees in the mountains of Lebanon for use in the construction of the Temple of Solomon. Due to excessive logging in Biblical times, this once-abundant tree is now uncommon in Lebanon.

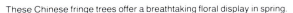

These Chinese fringe trees offer a breathtaking floral display in spring.

Chionanthus retusus. PSM 11

CHINESE FRINGE TREE.

Two different species, one native to China and the other to the eastern United States, comprise *Chionanthus.* The name is derived from the Greek words *chion,* meaning snow, and *anthos,* meaning flower, referring to the snow-white flowers that densely cover the tree in spring. This group planting of the Chinese variety, located in the parking lot of the Huntington Botanical Gardens in San Marino, contains impressive specimens noted for their size and esthetic quality. The trees are magnificent in April when their leafless branches are densely cloaked with ample clusters of sparkling white flowers.

MEXICAN HAND PLANT,
MONKEY FLOWER TREE,
DEVIL'S HAND-FLOWER TREE.

Native to Mexico, this evergreen tree was highly venerated in religious ceremonies by the Aztec Indians, who called it *macpalxochiquahuitl*. It is noted for its bizarre and sinister flowers, which somewhat resemble red fuzzy tulips. Projecting from the center of the cup of each is a structure resembling a withered, blood-red hand complete with fingernails, which is actually the reproductive portion of the flower. *Chiranthodendron* is named appropriately from three Greek words, *cheir,* meaning hand, *anthos,* meaning flower, and *dendron,* meaning tree. In Spanish it is called *arbol de las manitas,* tree of the little hands, or *mano de mico,* devil's hand. This extraordinary specimen, the largest in California, is located on the grounds of the Virginia Robinson Gardens in Beverly Hills.

This Mexican hand plant at the Virginia Robinson Gardens, has sinister-looking red flowers.

Chorisia has a bottle-shaped, moisture-storing trunk.

CHORISIA.

Chorisia is a small group of South American trees named in honor of Louis Choris, the scientific artist who in 1815 accompanied a Russian botanical expedition financed by Count Nikolai Romanzoff to Brazil and Argentina. *Chorisia* trees were discovered during the course of this expedition. This striking specimen is located on the east side of the Art Gallery at the Huntington Botanical Gardens in San Marino.

Called *yuchan* by local Indians or *palo borracho,* in Spanish meaning crazy tree or literally drunk stick, this tree is noted for its bottle-shaped trunk, wide and untapering along its lower portion, then narrowing to form a neck from which the branches spread. The tree occurs naturally in sparse woodlands where its moisture-storing trunk enables it to survive during the

(Chorisia insignis continued)

dry season. Adding to the uniqueness of the tree are the heavy, sharp spines densely studding the trunk and branches, showy pink to cream-colored flowers, and dangling fruits which split open and release a white cottony material considered a superior kapok substitute, used for stuffing cushions, pillows and life preservers. Its deciduous habit permits easy viewing of all these fantastic characteristics.

Chorisia speciosa. W 16
FLOSS-SILK TREE.

This specimen, on the grounds of the Hotel Bel-Air in the Bel-Air area of Los Angeles, is the single most spectacular flowering tree in the United States. This specimen was planted in 1915 by Ray Page, a member of the present Exceptional Trees of Los Angeles Committee. The largest of its kind in the United States — more than 90 feet tall with a trunk 13 feet around — its fruits and spiny character resemble those of its close relative, *C. insignis.* A native of southern Brazil and Argentina and called *samohu* by local Indians, it is a breathtaking sight in late summer when its bare branches are covered completely with showy pink flowers.

PASADENA PSM 4

Although not as large as the floss-silk tree at the Hotel Bel-Air, this tree is nevertheless noteworthy due to its location in the courtyard of the unique, Moorish style Pasadena City Hall. It is particulary striking when leafless in midwinter.

ARCADIA SGV 5

This group planting of floss-silk trees contains some of the largest and best-formed specimens in California. Located at the Los Angeles State and County Arboretum in Arcadia, they are a dramatic sight in late summer and early fall, when their pillar-like trunks are topped with a spreading crown of pink flowers.

A-C. *C. insignis* has a trunk heavily studded with sharp spines, creamed colored flowers, and fruits filled with a white cottony material.
D-F. The floss-silk tree at the Hotel Bel-Air, largest in the United States, has striking pink flowers, dangling, green fruit.
G. Another large floss-silk tree in a dramatic setting at the Moorish style Pasadena City Hall is leafless in winter.
H. The Arboretum in Arcadia has a big floss-silk tree.

Cinnamomum camphora.

CAMPHOR TREE.

Cinnamomum is named from the classical Greek word for cinnamon, *kinnamomum,* a species to which the camphor tree is closely related. Camphor gum and oil, used medicinally and industrially, are extracted from various parts of the tree. Although native to China and Japan, where its fragrant, insect-repelling wood is highly esteemed for cabinets and chests, the camphor tree is well-suited to the Los Angeles area. This imposing planting of well-maintained trees lines not-so-appropriately-named Maple Drive between Santa Monica and Sunset Boulevards in Beverly Hills.

The camphor becomes a large, spreading, handsome, well-structured tree with foliage that is pleasing to the eye year-round. Its leaves, a shiny yellow-green through winter, are replaced in spring by flushes of pink, red, or bronze growth, turning to an even more attractive, vibrant, shiny forest green. The trunk is dark, almost black when wet, contrasting dramatically with the lush, verdant new growth.

PASADENA   PSM 6

Pasadena is famous for its New Year's Day festivities marked by the traditional Tournament of Roses parade and Rose Bowl football game, but it should be equally famous for its camphor trees. More than 13,000 stately specimens line its streets. The most beautiful planting, composed of large, spreading trees that "kiss" as they meet over the street to create a tunnel-like effect, lines Ninita Parkway just east of the campus of the California Institute of Technology.

POMONA   SGV 28

Located in Pomona at 870 N. White Avenue, this is an exceptionally large and well-structured camphor tree. It is 60 feet tall, spreads nearly 80 feet, and has a trunk more than 13 feet around.

An imposing planting of well-maintained camphor trees lines Maple drive in Beverly Hills (upper) while a magnificent planting on Ninita Parkway in Pasadena (middle) touch over the street to create a tunnel-like effect. An exceptionally large camphor tree is in Pomona (bottom).

Members of the Southern California Gardeners' Federation stand beneath grapefruit they saved.

Cryptocarya rubra.   C 14
CRYPTOCARYA.

Cryptocarya, a group of about 250 trees and shrubs native mainly to tropical regions, is named from the Greek words *krypto,* meaning to hide, and *carya,* meaning walnut, referring to the concealed, walnut-like fruit of this species. A member of the laurel family and native to Chile, *C. rubra,* an evergreen, multi-trunked, handsomely shaped tree, is noted for its coppery red new foliage and attractive brown bark. In the Chilean province of Aconcagua, the oily seeds, after being cooked, serve as a source of food for the poorer classes. Rare in the landscape, this striking specimen in Elysian Park in Los Angeles is a remnant of the old Chavez Ravine Arboretum and is the largest of its kind in California.

Largest of its kind in California, this cryptocarya is in Elysian Park.

Citrus x paradisi.   C 5
GRAPEFRUIT.

About the middle of the last century, when Los Angeles was a sleepy pueblo, the area around Second and San Pedro Streets was planted in oranges, grapefruit, and lemons by John William Wolfskill and became the first commercial citrus grove in California. As Los Angeles spread outward from the old Plaza, bits and pieces of the grove were destroyed over the years to make way for commercial development. Finally, in 1980, the only remnant of the original citrus grove was a lone grapefruit tree situated behind a building on a vacant lot in what had become the Little Tokyo section of Los Angeles, the bustling and flourishing center of the Japanese-American community in Southern California.

The tree was destined for destruction in 1980 to make way for a parking garage when members of the Southern California Gardeners' Federation, a predominantly Japanese-American association, learned of its impending fate. Recognizing its historical and cultural significance, they spearheaded a community campaign to save the tree. Through the efforts and guidance of volunteers from the Southern California Gardeners' Federation, the tree was successfully dug, transported by crane, and then transplanted and reestablished in the plaza of the newly built Japanese-American Cultural and Community Center, where it serves as a living monument to the contributions made by Japanese immigrants to America.

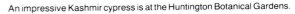

An impressive Kashmir cypress is at the Huntington Botanical Gardens.

The Guadalupe cypress is noted for its dark bluish foliage.

This Italian cypress was planted in 1850.

Cupressus cashmeriana.   PSM 13
KASHMIR CYPRESS.

Cupressus, a large group of conifers native around the world, is named from the Greek words *kus,* meaning to produce, and *parisos,* meaning equal, referring to the symmetrical growth habit characteristic of many of its species. This striking conifer, reputed to be the most beautiful and elegant of all cypresses, has ascending branches with remarkably pendulous branchlets and attractive gray-green foliage. It is native to the mountains of Afghanistan and Pakistan. Very rare in cultivation, this impressive specimen, located near the lily ponds at the Huntington Botanical Gardens in San Marino, is the largest of its kind in the United States.

Cupressus guadalupensis.   PSM 14
GUADALUPE CYPRESS.

The Guadalupe cypress is native to Guadalupe Island, off the west coast of Baja California in Mexico. Although once it formed extensive and dense stands, its reproduction has been halted by the grazing of goats released on the island. A beautiful tree noted for its dark bluish foliage and contrasting reddish-brown trunk and branches, it is perhaps the aristocrat of cypresses and would be more widely planted if better known. This specimen, located in the Huntington Botanical Gardens in San Marino, is exceptional because of its size and beauty.

Cupressus sempervirens.   S 2
ITALIAN CYPRESS.

In 1843, Jonathan Temple, a New Englander who operated a store in the Pueblo de Los Angeles, purchased the 27,000 acre Rancho Los Cerritos and built his adobe and redwood ranchhouse on gently rolling hills in what today is northwest Long Beach. Temple's rancho, originally part of a 1784 Spanish land grant, supported 15,000 head of cattle, 7,000 sheep, and 3,000 horses. Temple's interest in horticulture coupled with his desire to enhance esthetically the relatively barren grounds resulted in the development in about 1850 of an extensive Italian garden adjacent to the ranchhouse. He secured seeds of ornamental plants from friends in the eastern United States for planting in his garden. One of his original introductions, the Italian cypress, still stands in the remnants of his garden. It is a seldom-seen form with horizontal branches and dark green foliage, unlike the much more common stiff, upright, columnar selections with blue-green foliage.

Dalbergia sissoo.
SISSOO.

Dalbergia, a group of about 300 species of trees and shrubs including some of the true rosewoods highly esteemed for furniture, is native to northern India and the Himalayan region. The name honors the 18th-century Swedish botanist, Nicholas Dalberg, who was a plant collector in South America, and his brother, Carl. This imposing specimen, a rare member of the bean family and largest of its kind in California, is a remnant of the old Chavez Ravine Arboretum in Elysian Park in Los Angeles.

Sissoo, from an Indian name, is briefly deciduous in winter and one of the most valuable timbers of India. Also called shisham wood, it is used for furniture and flooring because of its resistance to termites and is highly prized for delicate earrings.

The largest giant dioon in California is more than 30 feet tall.

This sissoo, a rare member of the bean family, is in Elysian Park.

Dioon spinulosum.
GIANT DIOON.

The giant dioon is a member of the cycad group, popularly known as the living fossils because of their virtually unchanged form dating back to the Age of Dinosaurs. *Dioon* is named from the Greek words *dis,* meaning two, and *oon,* meaning egg, referring to the seeds being borne in pairs. Cycads are slow-growing, cone-bearing, woody plants that can live for hundreds of years.

This giant dioon, native to the tropical rain forests of Mexico where it was dug and removed in the early 1900s by Edward Howard for the famous plant collection of the Edward Doheny Estate, is the largest of its kind in California. It has a double-headed trunk more than 30 feet tall. Salvaged during the break-up of the Doheny Estate, it was replanted and now is adjacent to Rustic Canyon Recreation Center in the Pacific Palisades area of Los Angeles. This venerable, ancient specimen grows in the shade of a eucalyptus forest on the site of the Santa Monica Forestry Station, established in 1887 by the State Board of Forestry and the University of California as the first experimental forest site in the United States. Pioneering trials and evaluations of many exotic tree species, mainly *Eucalyptus,* were conducted there. A plaque marks the site as a state historical landmark.

Dombeya cacuminum.

STRAWBERRY SNOWBALL.

Named in honor of Joseph Dombey, 18th-century French botanist who accompanied a Spanish expedition to Peru and Chile, *Dombeya* is a group of showy-flowered trees and shrubs native to Africa and Madagascar. Located on the grounds of the Huntington Botanical Gardens in San Marino, this noteworthy specimen is the first and largest of its kind in California. Handsome in foliage, it is spectacular in January, when large, 1-foot clusters of pendulous coral-red flowers appear among the palmately pointed, tropical-looking leaves. Unlike other dombeyas, the flowers of the strawberry snowball drop cleanly, not persisting as unsightly, dried, brown clusters.

One of the largest in California, this strawberry snowball is spectacular in January with 1-foot clusters of coral-red flowers.

Impressive ear-pod trees at the Arboretum in Arcadia have spreading crowns, and curious, ear-shaped bean pods.

Enterolobium contortisiliquum.

EAR-POD TREE.

Enterolobium, a group of trees native to Central and South America, is named from the Greek words *enteron,* meaning intestine, and *lobos,* meaning lobe, referring to the shape of the fruits of some species. This member of the bean family, called "timbo colorado" or "pacara" in Spanish, is native to Brazil and Argentina, where it may attain immense dimensions, up to 100 feet tall with a 150-foot spread and a trunk several yards in diameter. Its wood and fruit contain saponin, a toxic glycoside that foams when put in water. This impressive specimen at the Los Angeles State and County Arboretum in Arcadia is a youngster at 30 years old but still spreads for more than 70 feet and has a trunk over 12 feet around. This handsome, wide-spreading, high crowned tree with delicate fern-like leaves occasionally bears curious, ear-shaped bean pods, hence the common name, ear-pod tree.

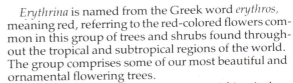

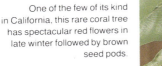

One of the few of its kind in California, this rare coral tree has spectacular red flowers in late winter followed by brown seed pods.

This well known planting of kaffirbooms colors Wilshire Boulevard in Santa Monica with scarlet flowers in late winter.

Erythrina abyssinica. W 38

CORAL TREE.

Erythrina is named from the Greek word *erythros,* meaning red, referring to the red-colored flowers common in this group of trees and shrubs found throughout the tropical and subtropical regions of the world. The group comprises some of our most beautiful and ornamental flowering trees.

This rare coral tree, native to eastern Africa, is the oldest and largest of the few of its kind existing in California. This striking tree, located at a private residence at the corner of Moore Street and Marco Place in the Mar Vista area of Los Angeles, is an easily observed spectacle when in full flower in late winter. As with most coral trees, it sheds its leaves just prior to flowering, resulting in a striking display of 6-inch clusters of peculiar red flowers borne prominently at the ends of leafless branches.

Erythrina caffra. W 31

KAFFIRBOOM, CORAL TREE.

More than 350 large kaffirbooms in a magnificent median planting occupy a 3-mile stretch of San Vicente Boulevard from near Wilshire Boulevard in Los Angeles to the Pacific Ocean in Santa Monica. A Historic-Cultural Monument of the City of Los Angeles, they are the largest planting of their kind in California. They are a beautiful sight in middle to late winter, when their nearly leafless branches carry showy terminal clusters of scarlet, keel-shaped flowers.

Erythrina crista-galli. C 8

COCKSPUR CORAL TREE.

Native to northern Argentina, Brazil, Paraguay, and Uruguay, where it is called "seibo," the cockspur coral tree occurs naturally along streams and water courses. This imposing tree is located in Heritage Square, a historical park dedicated to the preservation of buildings constructed in Los Angeles from 1875 to 1915 that exemplify the prominent architectural types of the Victorian Era.

Original buildings, rescued from demolition, have been brought together at this site next to Arroyo Seco just off the Pasadena Freeway at Avenue 43 in Los Angeles. Several of the structures are listed on the National Register of Historical Places and all have been designated Historic-Cultural Monuments by the City of Los Angeles. The Valley Knudsen Garden Residence, one of the few remaining examples of 19th-century Mansard architecture, was moved to the Square in 1971 to save it from demolition. This cockspur coral tree was moved along with the house from the original site and now thrives next to the residence.

This cockspur coral tree was moved along with the historic house behind it to its present location in Heritage Square.

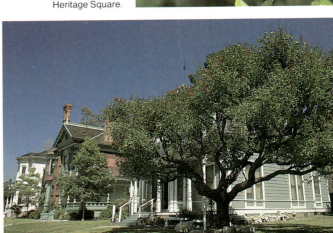

Erythrina falcata.   SGV 7
CORAL TREE.

Also called "seibo" and native from northern Argentina to Peru, this species of coral tree is one of the few evergreen types of *Erythrina*. If grown from seed, the tree may not bloom for 15 years or more, although it flowers much sooner when grown from cuttings of wood from mature trees. Unlike some of the other coral trees which flower when leafless, this particular species has flowers and leaves together. Although a relative youngster, this coral tree in the Los Angeles State and County Arboretum in Arcadia is the largest in California. A striking sight in late spring or early summer, the tree's floral display promises to become even showier as the tree becomes older.

GRIFFITH PARK   C 21

Rare in the landscape, this impressive planting of coral trees in the median along the 2500 block of Vermont Avenue near the entrance to Griffith Park in Los Angeles consists of 18 of the largest trees of their kind in California.

The Arboretum in Arcadia is home to this large, impressive *E. falcata.*

This impressive planting of 18 *E. falcata* near Griffith Park has a fine display of red flowers in May.

E. speciosa, an anomaly among coral trees because of the hollow twigs and stalks which hold its leaflets, has an unusual, stunning flower cluster.

Erythrina speciosa.   W 21
CORAL TREE.

In its native Brazil, this striking, small tree usually occurs in swampy ground and along water courses. It is an anomaly among coral trees because of the hollow twigs and stalks which hold its leaflets. Rare in the landscape, this exceptional specimen at a private residence in the 1200 block of Amalfi Drive in the Pacific Palisades area of Los Angeles is a stunning sight when in flower in spring.

Eucalyptus amplifolia.   W 35
CABBAGE GUM.

Cabbage gums are noted for their ash-white, smooth trunks. This planting in Santa Monica is the largest in number and size in California.

Eucalyptus is named from the Greek words *eu,* meaning well, and *kalyptos,* meaning covered, referring to a cap that tightly seals the flower when in bud. The genus *Eucalyptus* includes more than 600 species of trees and shrubs mostly native to Australia. Due to their fast rate of growth, useful timber, ornamental value, and ability to grow where subject to such adverse conditions as heat, drought, wind, and poor soil, eucalypts have been widely planted in warmer areas around the globe. Eucalypts have been in the California landscape for more than 100 years and have done exceedingly well here. In fact, more kinds of eucalypts are growing in Southern California than anywhere else except Australia. They almost appear to be native California trees.

This striking planting of cabbage gums, consisting of 18 trees along Stewart Street between Delaware and Kansas Avenues in Santa Monica, is the largest in number and size of trees of their kind in California. These rare trees are noted for their ash-white, smooth trunks, several of which are more than 60 feet tall.

Eucalyptus citriodora.   PSM 33
LEMON-SCENTED GUM.

As written on the sign, this lemon-scented gum in South Pasadena was planted by John Muir in 1889.

This species of eucalypt receives its name from its leaves, which when crushed give off a strong and pleasant lemon scent. It is also one of the most handsome eucalypts with its graceful, slender, white to pink smooth-barked trunk supporting a lacy, open crown of light green, sickle-shaped leaves. This particular specimen was planted in 1889 by John Muir, noted naturalist and conservationist, at the Wynyate residence in South Pasadena, home of the first mayor of that city.

COVINA   SGV 30

More than 100 feet tall with a trunk 13 feet around, this handsome lemon-scented gum is the largest of its kind in the area. It is located at the corner of Grand Avenue and Puente Street in Covina.

This lemon-scented gum in Covina is one of the largest in California.

Eucalyptus deanei. W 33
DEAN'S GUM.

This rare and striking eucalypt is in front of a residence at 522 24th Street in Santa Monica. It was planted in the early 1920s by Hugh Evans of Evans and Reeves Nursery who introduced many exotic plants into the Los Angeles landscape. Only a few specimens of this exceedingly handsome tree exist in California. More than 100 feet tall, this is the tallest and most massive tree of its kind in the United States.

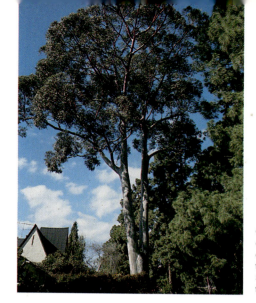

Only a few specimens of Dean's gum, an exceedingly handsome tree, exist in the United States. This is the tallest.

Eucalyptus deglupta. W 11
MINDANAO GUM.

One of the few eucalypts indigenous to wet tropical forests, the Mindanao gum can attain immense proportions in its natural habitat. In New Guinea and on Mindanao Island in the Philippines, where the trees are native, they may become 200 feet tall with trunks more than 25 feet around. Although this planting on the east side of the medical center on the UCLA campus in the Westwood area of Los Angeles does not consist of trees this large, these specimens are exceptional due to their rarity and handsome, slightly buttressed trunks with smooth bark peeling away to reveal longitudinal patches of various shades of green, orange, and brown.

One of the few tropical eucalypts, the Mindanao gum has smooth bark peeling in shades of green, orange, brown.

Eucalyptus diversicolor. W 25
KARRI GUM.

The karri gum, one of the tallest eucalypts, is native to southwestern Australia. Its bark is an excellent source of tannin used in the tanning process to increase the durability, moisture resistance, and flexibility of animal skins. It is rare in cultivation, this being one of the few specimens in the United States. This exceptional tree is located near the drinking fountain at the north end of Palisades Park in Santa Monica.

The karri gum, one of the tallest eucalypts and hardwoods known, is rare in cultivation. This is one of the few specimens in the United States.

Eucalyptus ficifolia. S 8
RED-FLOWERING GUM.

Perhaps the showiest of all eucalypts, the red-flowering gum is noted for its stunning displays of pink, rose, orange, scarlet, or crimson flowers in 1-foot clusters profusely covering trees in summer. It is one of the best flowering trees for coastal areas, where it attains its maximum beauty. This exceptionally well-shaped and -maintained orange-flowered specimen is located at 712 Broadway in Redondo Beach. It is more than 40 feet tall, spreads 50 feet, and has a trunk 13 feet around.

The red-flowering gum, noted for its lavish, summer flowers and cup-like fruits, does best in coastal areas.

Eucalyptus globulus. SFV 4
BLUE GUM.

Perhaps no other eucalypt is as characteristic of the Southern California skyline or landscape as the blue gum. Blue gums at Shadow Ranch, a city park in the Canoga Park area of Los Angeles in the San Fernando Valley, are reported to be the parent trees of the blue gums so common in Southern California. They were planted in the 1870s by Albert Workman, ranch superintendent for Isaac Lankershim and I. N. Van Nuys, whose company produced wheat on the 60,000-acre site. Workman, who purchased part of the site to build a ranch house, arranged for the trees to be brought by boat from his native Australia. Four of the original trees near the restored ranch house now have trunks more than 20 feet around, the largest being 25 feet around and more than 100 feet tall.

ARCADIA SGV 8

This huge blue gum was probably planted by E. J. "Lucky" Baldwin over 100 years ago on his estate, known as Rancho Santa Anita, site of the present-day Los Angeles State and County Arboretum in Arcadia. The tree is located next to Baldwin's ornate Queen Anne Cottage.

Much of our California heritage is reflected in the Arboretum. Gabrielino Indians were first attracted to the area by the spring-fed lake, plant life, and abundant game. In the early 1800s the site became the center of Rancho Santa Anita, a 13,000-acre grant belonging to Mission San Gabriel. In the 1840s a Scotsman, Hugo Reid, obtained title to the Rancho and after passing through several hands and being reduced in size, it was finally bought in 1875 by Baldwin, a flamboyant entrepreneur and millionaire.

Baldwin recognized the Rancho's financial potential and built it into a 50,000-acre agricultural empire. He

This blue gum at Shadow Ranch is well over 100 years old, has delicate, white flowers.

founded the city of Arcadia and developed the first horse-racing track there, the precursor of today's well-known Santa Anita Racetrack. In addition, he was responsible for contracting the Santa Fe Railway to construct a depot, now restored on the Arboretum grounds, on Rancho Santa Anita at which he could order all trains stopped at his will. Restored on the Arboretum grounds not far from this blue gum are the Hugo Reid Adobe and Baldwin's ornate Queen Anne Cottage and Coach Barn. These latter two serve as reminders, along with the numerous and conspicuous peafowl that inhabit the Arboretum grounds, of Baldwin's reputation for extravagant taste and lavish entertainment.

Eucalyptus grandis.   W 12
ROSE GUM.

Attesting to the species unusually fast rate of growth, this towering specimen in the Mildred E. Mathias Botanical Garden at UCLA in the Westwood area of Los Angeles is less than 30 years old but is almost 125 feet tall with a trunk 10 feet around. One of the most handsome of all eucalypts, the rose gum is noted for its clean, tall, powder-white, marble-column-like trunk, and dark green foliage.

Eucalyptus tereticornis.   S 7
FOREST RED GUM.

Of the many trees from throughout the world planted by transportation king General Phineas Banning around his mansion in the 1860s, this forest red gum, 90 feet tall and with a trunk over 13 feet around, is the largest. Banning grew this tree from seed given him by a missionary returning from Australia.

Although arriving in Los Angeles in 1851, virtually penniless at the age of 21, Banning quickly established himself on the transportation scene through ownership of a railroad, freight lines, and a fleet of ships. Regarded as the "father of Los Angeles Harbor," he cofounded the town of New San Pedro, later renamed Wilmington after Banning's birthplace in Delaware, and was a state senator and community leader. He encouraged the Southern Pacific Railroad to construct a line into Los Angeles. Banning built his home in 1864 to provide himself with a view of the harbor and approaching ships. Today the restored mansion and grounds are the centerpiece of Banning Park in the Wilmington area of Los Angeles not far from Los Angeles Harbor.

This blue gum was planted by "Lucky" Baldwin over 100 years ago.

A towering rose gum at UCLA is less than 30 years old.

This forest red gum was grown from seed brought by a missionary returning from Australia.

Ficus benghalensis.   SE 12
BANYAN FIG.

Ficus is a large group of from 1500 to 2000 species of woody plants, mainly trees, native to warm regions of the globe. When cut or wounded, they exude a white, milky sap in a manner similar to that of the true rubber tree. Hence, they are often referred to as rubber plants although they are not closely related to the true rubber tree. The common name of this species was given by the British in reference to the banyans or banians, Hindu traders of India where the tree is native, who used the space under the tree's spreading branches as a marketplace.

The banyan is especially noted for the abundance of aerial roots originating from the undersides of the branches and growing downward to the ground, forming props or auxiliary trunks that serve as supports for the spreading branches. In the tropics, banyans can attain immense proportions by this habit of spreading branches and dropping aerial roots. One tree in India is said to have measured 2,000 feet around its crown and to have cast a shadow covering more than an acre. Due to the lack of sustained, high humidity and warmth, the few banyan trees in California will never reach such a large size or develop the abundant aerial roots characteristic of this tropical tree. The extraordinary banyan planted in 1904 in front of the Fred C. Nelles State School, a California Historical Landmark in Whittier, is the largest of its kind in California. It is nearly 50 feet tall, spreads 60 feet, and has a trunk over 8 feet around with a few hanging aerial roots that have not yet reached the ground.

This extraordinary banyan fig was planted in 1904.

The patriarch of all Moreton Bay figs is in Glendora.

A big Indian rubber tree with spreading roots is in San Dimas.

Ficus elastica 'Decora'.   SGV 25
INDIAN RUBBER TREE.

This horticultural variety, a type used commonly in the indoor house plant trade, is the largest of its kind in the Los Angeles area. The tree is located next to the old Teague Ranch residence at 117 Fifth Street in San Dimas. The Teague family was prominent in citrus farming when the San Dimas area was a center of citrus production, particularly of lemons. The tree is more than 40 feet tall and has roots that have spread under the house and surfaced on the other side, more than 50 feet away.

Ficus macrophylla.

MORETON BAY FIG.

The Moreton Bay fig is native to Queensland and northern New South Wales in Australia. There its 1-inch, globular, purple fruit are much sought after as food by bats, or flying foxes, as these winged mammals are popularly called. Of the dozen Moreton Bay fig trees designated as exceptional, this specimen located in Fig Tree Park at the corner of Colorado and Santa Fe Avenues in Glendora is the patriarch of them all. In fact, this specimen is the most massive cultivated tree in the greater Los Angeles area, surpassing an even more famous tree of the same kind at the railroad station in Santa Barbara. It is close to 100 years old and nearly 100 feet tall, spreads over more than 1/4 acre, and has a trunk that is an astounding 34 1/2 feet around. Like all other Moreton Bay figs, this specimen is noted for its massive buttressed roots, which spread for many feet out from the trunk.

WEST LOS ANGELES W 36

This magnificent, spreading Moreton Bay fig specimen is located on the grounds of St. John's Church near the corner of National Boulevard and Military Avenue in west Los Angeles. More than 100 years old, it is a Historic-Cultural Monument of the City of Los Angeles.

SANTA MONICA W 30

Another spreading giant, this Moreton Bay fig is situated attractively on the grounds of the Miramar Hotel on Ocean Avenue near Wilshire Boulevard in Santa Monica. It was planted in 1879 by the flamboyant, long-time Nevada senator, John Percival Jones, who had numerous financial dealings and land holdings in the Santa Monica area.

SANTA MONICA W 23

Planted in 1913 from a 2-pound coffee can by the Caldwell family, who are still the owners, this Moreton Bay fig tree with huge spreading buttresses is now a giant covering a large portion of the backyard of the 236 Adelaide Drive residence in Santa Monica. It is best viewed from the alley behind the house.

SANTA MONICA W 32

This parkway planting, a most unusual use for these trees considering their massive buttresses and surface rooting habit, is in the 1900-to-2600 blocks of La Mesa Drive in Santa Monica. Although not as massive as most of the other notable Moreton Bay figs, these trees

A large Moreton Bay fig is at St. John's Church in west Los Angeles.

A Moreton Bay fig is situated attractively at the Miramar Hotel.

Moreton Bay figs in Santa Monica: A large specimen (above) at the Caldwell residence, (below) along La Mesa Drive.

(*Ficus macrophylla*, Moreton Bay fig continued)

are nevertheless large, well-maintained, and of superb conformation. The crowns of trees on both sides of La Mesa Drive intermingle over the center of the street creating a tunnel-like effect. The buttressed roots snaking their way 20 or 30 feet along a curb or sidewalk are an unusual sight.

OLVERA STREET   C 7

This group planting of Moreton Bay figs dates to the 1870s and is located in El Pueblo de Los Angeles State Historic Park around the old plaza near Olvera Street, formerly the town square. They are some of the first of their kind planted in California and the first trees planted in El Pueblo.

The Pueblo is the site of early Los Angeles where in 1781 44 "pobladores" acting on the orders of the King of Spain established a farming community in order to colonize this area of California. Since that time, Los Angeles has grown and developed into one of the world's largest metropolitan areas. The history of the area immediately surrounding El Pueblo reflects the heritage and contributions of the Hispanic, Black, Italian, French, Anglo, German, and Chinese immigrants to the growth and development of Los Angeles.

BEVERLY HILLS   W 8

Located in the forest of king palms in the Virginia Robinson Gardens in Beverly Hills, this Moreton Bay fig is exceptional due to the unusual and extensive root system that originates from its upper trunk and drops more than 20 feet through the air into the ground. These aerial roots are characteristic of some trees growing in damp, humid, shady, usually tropical environments. Their development in an arid, less tropical environment such as Southern California is a rare phenomenon.

DOWNEY   SE 4
(Not Pictured)

This impressive Moreton Bay fig, one of the largest of its kind in the county, is at Rancho Los Amigos Hospital in Downey.

LONG BEACH   S 1

These two spreading Moreton Bay figs standing on either side of the front entrance to the ranch house at Rancho Los Alamitos in Long Beach were planted in the 1890s by Susan Bixby, wife of owner John Bixby. Bixby, a member of one of the more prominent of the early pioneering families in the Long Beach area, was the owner most responsible for the development of the Italian theme gardens surrounding the Rancho. The two trees dwarf the house, one of the few structures standing in California that has existed under the Spanish, Mexican, and American flags. The Rancho, originally part of the same 18th-century Spanish land grant that gave rise to Rancho Los Cerritos, was used primarily for sheep and cattle and in later years for agronomic crops.

36

A historic group of Moreton Bay figs is near Olvera Street.

This Moreton Bay fig in Beverly Hills has an unusual development of aerial roots.

Two Moreton Bay figs guard the ranch house at Rancho Los Alamitos, Long Beach.

An atypical, wind-swept, flat crown and trunk with a long slit-like "window" characterize this Moreton Bay fig in Redondo Beach.

REDONDO BEACH   S 9

Although not as large as the other exceptional
Moreton Bay figs, this is still a specimen worthy of
such recognition. It is located at the south end of the
library in Veterans' Park in Redondo Beach, a short
distance from a bluff overlooking the Pacific Ocean.
Here, it has been buffeted for years by brisk ocean
breezes, which have given it an uncharacteristic lean-
ing, wind-swept, high, flat-crowned form. Just as unusual are its two parallel trunks that arise together,
separate, and then merge again to form a long slit-like
"window" in the trunk.

LOS ANGELES   C 3

This imposing Moreton Bay fig specimen guards the
entrance to the headquarters of the Automobile Club
of Southern California at the corner of Figueroa Street
and Adams Boulevard in Los Angeles. For more than
80 years the Club has had a profound impact on the
development of suburbs and the role of the auto in the
Southern California lifestyle by encouraging and supporting construction and maintenance of an extensive
network of roads and freeways. Planted about 1900 on
the grounds of one of the residences in what is referred
to as the West Adams district, it is as tall as the five-
story Auto Club buildings that now flank it on either
side. This exceptional tree is one of the more than a
dozen old Moreton Bay figs clustered in the West
Adams area. They are remnant plantings of the large
residences of this once most exclusive and affluent
neighborhood.
The West Adams area contained the homes of such
well known families as Doheny, W. J. Davis, Hancock,
Banning, W. F. Cline, and General Longstreet. Several
of the homes, some of them outstanding examples of
turn-of-the-century architecture, remain in the area.

SAN MARINO   PSM 16

These three trees at the Huntington Botanical
Gardens in San Marino are a distinct form of the
Moreton Bay fig and the only three of their kind in
California. Native to tiny Lord Howe Island off the
coast of Australia, this form is noted for its tall, columnar trunk rather than the spreading, massive, multi-
branched trunks characteristic of the more common
form. This handsome columnar form should be more
widely used and would be a striking addition to parks
or other large open landscape areas.

PASADENA   PSM 5

Located on South Marengo Avenue north of
Cordova Street in Pasadena, this imposing Moreton
Bay fig was planted in 1880 by Thomas Early to provide
shade for his garden and house. During his term as
mayor of Pasadena, from 1907 to 1914, Early once
entertained President William Howard Taft at his
home. The city of Pasadena eventually obtained title to
Early's property and in the 1970s constructed a confer-
ence facility known as the Pasadena Center on the site.
During the construction of the center the tree was
saved and insured for $15,000 by the city.

An imposing Moreton
Bay fig guards the
entrance to the
headquarters of the
Southern California
Automobile Club.

This handsome
columnar form of
Moreton Bay figs in San
Marino should be more
widely planted in large
landscape areas.

During construction of
the Pasadena Center,
the city insured this
Moreton Bay fig, below,
for $15,000.

Ficus religiosa.
C 16
BO TREE, PEEPUL.

A native of India, the bo tree has been venerated above all other trees by Buddhists because Siddhartha Gautama, founder and leader of the Buddhist religion, was said to have been sitting under such a tree when he became "enlightened" or achieved perfect knowledge. Rare in California, this exceptional specimen is a remnant of the old Chavez Ravine Arboretum in Elysian Park in Los Angeles. With a multi-branched trunk over 16 feet around, it is the largest of its kind in California.

The veneration given it by the people of India is reflected in their saying "It is better to die a leper than pluck a leaf of a peepul." Linné, the great Swedish botanist and naturalist who named the tree, felt it was so sacred to Indians that he described the species as the "religious tree," hence the name *religiosa*. Bo trees can attain enormous size and live for hundreds of years. A bo tree sent from India to Anuradhapura in Ceylon and planted in 288 B.C. is the oldest cultivated living tree known.

This rare bo tree is in Elysian Park.

Ficus retusa.
W 3
INDIAN LAUREL.

Native to the Malay Peninsula and Borneo, the Indian laurel has become one of the most common parkway and street trees in Southern California. Of the several forms available, the most handsome and most resistant to the leaf-rolling Cuban laurel thrip that plagues the trees throughout the area is the one with broadly ovate leaves.

This outstanding parkway planting on Rodeo Drive in Beverly Hills is unsurpassed for number, conformation, and beauty of trees. Rodeo Drive, home to some of the most affluent shops and restaurants in the world, is frequented by the rich and famous.

A parkway planting of Indian laurels lines Rodeo Drive in Beverly Hills.

The largest planting of rusty-leaved figs is at UCLA.

Ficus rubiginosa.
W 13
RUSTY-LEAVED FIG.

UCLA in the Westwood area of Los Angeles is the home of this splendid planting of rusty-leaved figs. More than 20 large, handsome, well-formed, dome-shaped trees line either side of Dickson Court, near the center of the campus. This planting is an outstanding example of the landscape value of this species and demonstrates that it is worthy of more widespread planting as an ornamental.

Ficus sycomorus. SGV 9
SYCAMORE FIG.

The name sycamore is derived from the Greek words, "sykon," meaning fig, and "moron," meaning mulberry, hence the species is commonly called the mulberry fig. It is native to the Arabian Peninsula, the Holy Land, and Egypt. This magnificent specimen with a trunk 10 feet around is at at the Los Angeles State and County Arboretum in Arcadia. It is the largest of its kind in California.

Considered a sacred tree in its native lands, the sycamore fig is figured on the walls of a temple at Karnak as dedicated to Hathor, approximately equivalent to the Greek Aphrodite. It is the sycamore referred to in the Bible on several occasions. In the popular Biblical story, Zacchaeus climbed a sycamore fig in order to see Jesus pass by. So valuable was the tree to ancient Jews that King David appointed a special overseer for the trees as he did for olives. The fruits of the sycamore were used extensively for food by the poor and nomads.

The sycamore fig is notable, also, for its cauliflorous fruiting habit, a reference to the production of flowers and fruits borne profusely on short, forked twigs in dense clusters directly from the trunk and larger branches, a peculiarity shared with other species of *Ficus*.

F. thonningii at the Huntinton Botanical Gardens are rare.

Ficus thonningii. PSM 17
FICUS.

This native of Tropical West Africa, where it is common and considered a stately shade tree, is rare in the United States. These extraordinary specimens providing shade for the Jungle Garden at the Huntington Botanical Gardens in San Marino are the largest of their kind in California. Several are 75 feet tall and have trunks 15 feet around.

Fraxinus velutina var. *coriacea.*

LEATHERLEAF ASH, MONTEBELLO ASH.

(Not Pictured)

Although indigenous to Southern California, the leatherleaf ash is not at all common here. This remarkable specimen, one of the largest seen, has a trunk nearly 7 feet around. It is on the west side of the main house on Strauss Ranch off Mulholland Highway near Kanan Road, an area to be included in the Santa Monica Mountains Recreation Area.

Ginkgo biloba. SGV 27

MAIDENHAIR TREE.

This impressive maidenhair tree is particularly striking around the 1st of December, when its leaves have changed from green to a bright golden yellow and are just beginning to carpet the ground.

Rare in its native habitat in Chekiang province in China, *Ginkgo* is derived from a Chinese name for the trees. The tree was thought to be extinct in the wild until it was rediscovered in 1916 by Frank Meyers, plant explorer for the United States Department of Agriculture. This impressive specimen at 1180 N. Palomares Street in Pomona is 70 feet tall and has a trunk more than 8 feet around. In excellent condition and with outstanding form, it is particularly striking about the 1st of December, when its leaves have changed from green to a bright golden yellow and are just beginning to carpet the ground.

The ginkgo is not a flowering plant but a gymnosperm and a relic species whose leaves from millions of years ago have been found fossilized. The maidenhair tree qualifies along with the cycads and ferns as one of the longest-surviving vascular plants. They existed in the Jurassic period, 180 million years ago when dinosaurs ruled the earth, the Sierra Nevada Mountains and their gold were being formed, and birds and mammals were beginning to evolve.

Maidenhair trees are dioecious; that is, individual trees are either male or female. Since female trees produce fruits with foul-smelling pulp, it is recommended that male trees be selected for planting as ornamentals. Cleaned seeds are pure white and sold for food in China and Japan, where the kernels are eaten at banquets, weddings, and other special social gatherings.

Grevillea robusta.
SILK OAK.

Named in honor of Charles Francis Greville, 18th-century plantsman, founder and vice-president of the Royal Horticultural Society in England, *Grevillea* includes about 200 species of trees and shrubs native mainly to Australia. Planted about 1900 in front of the Fred C. Nelles State School in Whittier and now almost 90 feet tall with a trunk 10 feet around, this imposing specimen is one of the largest and best-formed silk oaks in the area. A member of the protea family and not a true oak, it is noted for its attractive, pinnately divided leaves and showy, 6- to 10-inch, comb-like tresses of orange-yellow flowers that appear along nearly leafless branches in early summer.

One of the largest and best-formed in the area, this silk oak in noted for its attractive, pinnately divided leaves and showy, comb-like tresses of orange-yellow flowers in early summer.

Harpullia pendula.   W 14
TULIPWOOD.

Harpullia, a Latinized name of Indian origin, comprises about 35 species of trees native from India to Australia and the Pacific Islands. It is a member of the soapberry family, which includes such well-known tropical fruits as the litchi and rambutan. This extraordinary specimen, a native of Australia, is in the Court of Sciences, against the Mathematics Building, at UCLA in the Westwood area of Los Angeles. It was introduced to Southern California in the 1930s by Hugh Evans of Evans and Reeves Nursery. The largest of its kind in California, its pinnate, glossy, bright green leaves are a handsome complement to the ever present, tangerine orange, leathery, inflated capsules that split to reveal shiny, jet-black seeds.

An impressive tulipwood at UCLA has handsome, glossy, bright green leaves complemented by ever present, tangerine orange, leathery, inflated capsules that split to reveal shiny, jet-black seeds.

Jacaranda mimosifolia.
JACARANDA.

Native to Central and South America, *Jacaranda* is a Latinized Brazilian name for a group of trees characterized by showy flowers and finely divided, fern-like foliage. This particular species, a native of southern Brazil and northern Argentina, is one of the most commonly planted landscape trees in the area. Used extensively in street-tree plantings and noted for their showy terminal clusters of blue tubular flowers borne on leafless branches, they paint the horizon in a sea of blue during peak flowering in early summer. This notable parkway planting, unsurpassed in number, size, and shapeliness of trees, covers several residential blocks including Carnell and LaForge Streets and Flomar Drive between Gunn and Mills Avenues in southeastern Whittier.

A notable, extensive parkway planting of jacarandas is in Whittier. Finely divided, fern-like foliage is a nice complement to blue flowers.

SAN MARINO   PSM 32

Nearly 50 feet tall and with a spread over 50 feet, this handsome, dome-shaped jacaranda tree at 1870 Los Robles Avenue in San Marino is the largest and most outstanding specimen in the area.

This 100-year-old black walnut still produces fruit at the Arboretum in Arcadia.

A handsome, dome-shaped jacaranda in San Marino is the largest and most outstanding specimen in the area. Showy, tubular, blue flowers appear in early summer.

Juglans nigra.
BLACK WALNUT.

Juglans, the ancient Latin name for the Persian walnut, is named from *jovis,* meaning of Jupiter, and *glans,* meaning an acorn, referring to the walnut being the acorn of the god Jupiter. Closely related to the Persian walnut, these 100-year-old black walnuts, some more than 75 feet tall, are the remnants of a grove planted by E.J. "Lucky" Baldwin not far from his home on his estate, Rancho Santa Anita, site of the present day Los Angeles State and County Arboretum in Arcadia.

Juglans 'Paradoxa'.   SE 13
PARADOX WALNUT.

This tree, a hybrid between the English or Persian walnut and a native California walnut, was planted in 1907 by the University of California Agriculture Experiment Station in Whittier, an early center of walnut production in Southern California. Designated as a California Historical Landmark, it is on Whittier Boulevard near Penn Street along what was once originally a section of El Camino Real, the King's Highway, the route linking the Spanish missions throughout California in the 1700s and 1800s. Having withstood several attempts to have it destroyed in order to widen Whittier Boulevard, the tree has grown to massive size with a spread of more than 100 feet and a trunk 14 feet around.

A tremendous keteleeria at the Huntinton Botanical Gardens has upright, woody cones and linear, glossy leaves.

This paradox walnut has a massive branching structure that is best viewed in winter when deciduous.

Keteleeria davidiana.   PSM 18
KETELEERIA.

The name *Keteleeria* honors Jean Baptiste Keteler, a 19th-century Belgian-born French horticulturist. Growing up to 100 feet tall and native to mountains of China and Taiwan where it was once abundant but is now uncommon, this member of the pine family has upright, woody cones with persistent scales and linear, glossy leaves. This tremendous specimen, reputed to be the largest of its kind in the United States, is at the Huntington Botanical Gardens in San Marino.

Kigelia pinnata.
SAUSAGE TREE.

Kigelia is a Latinized African vernacular name for this tree, a native of Tropical West Africa. It is one of the most curious of trees because it produces strange, large, sausage-shaped fruits which dangle below the branches on thin cord-like stems as long as 5 feet, giving it the appearance of an outdoor delicatessen. This outstanding specimen, one of the largest of its kind in the United States and one of a few in California, is behind Murphy Hall at UCLA in the Westwood area of Los Angeles. It has a trunk more than 6 feet around, is more than 30 feet tall, and spreads 40 feet.

In its native land the seeds are roasted and eaten and its baked fruit is used for fermenting beer. The fruit is also used medicinally for treatment of ulcers, stomach ailments, venereal diseases, and rheumatism. Preceding the persistent, sausage-shaped fruits are 6-inch, blackish-red, bell-shaped flowers. These unpleasant-smelling, night-blooming flowers are pollinated by bats.

A large sausage tree at UCLA has pendulous, sausage-shaped fruits and blackish-red, bat-pollinated flowers.

This magnificent cow-itch has outstanding form and pale pink to rose-purple flowers.

Lagunaria patersonii. W 2
COW-ITCH.

The name Lagunaria honors Andrea de Laguna, 15th Century Spanish botanist and physician to Pope Julius III. This evergreen member of the hibiscus family and Australian native is noted for its attractive, cup-shaped, pale pink to rose-purple flowers up to 3 inches across that profusely cover the trees in early summer. Five-parted seed capsules covered with irritating, needle-like hairs follow the flowers. This magnificent specimen, in front of a residence on Bedford Drive near Elevado Avenue in Beverly Hills, is noted for its outstanding form and 70-foot height, making it one of the largest in California.

The Australian tea tree is noted for its twisted, deeply furrowed, gray-brown, sprawling trunks.

Leptospermum laevigatum.

AUSTRALIAN TEA TREE.

Leptospermum is named from the Greek words *leptos,* meaning thin, and *sperma,* meaning seed, referring to its tiny, thin seeds. A native of Australia, its leaves and those of similar species were used to brew tea, hence the common name. The great 18th-century English explorer and navigator Captain James Cook used this tea to control scurvy among his crew. A member of the eucalyptus family, the Australian tea tree is noted for its picturesque, almost sculptured habit of twisted, muscular-looking, deeply furrowed, shaggy, gray-brown trunks and branches that sprawl along the ground for some distance. This extraordinary specimen, overlooking the ocean near the southern end of Palisades Park in Santa Monica, has twisted, serpentine trunks undulating across the ground more than 30 feet.

Liquidambar styraciflua.　　　SGV 1

LIQUIDAMBAR, AMERICAN SWEET GUM.

Liquidambar is one of the most dependable trees for good autumn foliage color in coastal Southern California, has curious spiny fruits.

Liquidambar is named from the Latin words *liquidus,* meaning liquid, and *ambar,* meaning amber, referring to the fragrant resin produced by these trees. The American sweet gum, a source of the commercially important aromatic balsam called styrax, used in medicine and perfume, is a native of the Eastern United States. In Southern California it is one of our most dependable trees for good autumn foliage color. This splendid parkway planting, unsurpasssed for size and form of trees and brilliance of fall color, is on Ross Avenue in Alhambra.

Liriodendron tulipifera. SE 5

TULIP TREE.

Liriodendron is named from the Greek words *leirion,* meaning lily, and *dendron,* meaning tree, referring to the shape of the tree's flowers. One of the noblest of American trees, the tulip tree is native to forests of the Eastern United States. Specimens up to 200 feet tall have been recorded with handsome, columnar trunks unbranched for a considerable distance. Scattered among the broadly lobed, light green leaves in late spring and early summer are greenish-yellow, tulip-like flowers with a broad orange band at their base. This planting along the 5400 block of Rockne Avenue in Whittier is exceptional for size and number of trees.

One of the noblest of American trees, the tulip tree has handsome, columnar trunks, broadly lobed leaves, tulip-like flowers, good autumn color.

An unsurpassed, formal planting of fountain palms is at the Huntington Botanical Gardens.

Livistona decipiens. PSM 19

FOUNTAIN PALM.

Livistona, a group of about 30 species of fan palms native from Tropical Asia to Australia, is named in honor of Patrick Murray, Baron of Liviston, whose extensive collection of plants became the basis of the famous Royal Botanic Gardens in Edinburgh, Scotland. This Australian native is noted for its deeply divided, fan-shaped leaves. The leaves' great number of pendulous, wavering segments give a fountain-like effect to the tree's crown. Uncommon in cultivation, this imposing planting in a formal section of the Huntington Botanical Gardens in San Marino is outstanding for the number and size of trees.

Lonchocarpus nitidus. W 17

LONCHOCARPUS.

Lonchocarpus is named from the Greek words *lonche,* meaning lance, and *karpos,* meaning fruit, referring to the shape of the fruit. It includes about 100 species of trees in the bean family native to tropical America, Africa, and Australia. This particular species, native to South America and called ''yerba de bugre'' in Argentina, yields a valuable and durable wood. Rare in cultivation, this handsome, blue-flowered tree is on the grounds of the Hotel Bel-Air in the Bel-Air area of Los Angeles. It is the largest of its kind in the United States.

This handsome, blue-flowered lonchocarpus, rare in cultivation, is at the Hotel Bel-Air.

An impressive Brisbane box at Greystone Park in Beverly Hills has curiously fringed flower parts.

Lophostemon confertus. W 5

BRISBANE BOX.

Lophostemon is named from the Greek words *lophis,* meaning crest, and *stemon,* meaning stamen, referring to the fringed stamens (male reproductive organs) of the tree's flowers. Until recently included in the genus *Tristania,* the Brisbane box is a close relative of the eucalypts and noted for its handsome, smooth, reddish-brown bark and attractive leaves. This outstanding tree, perhaps the largest and finest of its kind in California, is on the grounds of Greystone Park in Beverly Hills.

It was probably planted in the 1920s by Edward L. Doheny, millionaire oilman, near the house that he built and gave as a gift to his only son, Edward L. Doheny, Jr. Built at a cost of $4 million, about $40 million in today's money, castle-like Greystone Mansion contains 55 rooms and over an acre of floor space. Today, the mansion and grounds are a public park of Beverly Hills.

One of the first introduced to California, this macadamia nut has white flowers occurring in long, pendulous clusters.

Magnolia delavayi.   PSM 21

DELAVAY MAGNOLIA.

Magnolia, a group of trees and large shrubs with spectacular, showy flowers, is named in honor of Pierre Magnol, 17th-century horticulturist and director of the botanic garden in Montpellier, France. The magnolia family is considered by botanists to be among the most primitive of flowering plants. Native to southwestern China and rare in the landscape, this is one of the few evergreen cultivated magnolias. It is noted for its tropical-looking leaves that are up to 14 inches long and 8 inches wide and its 6-inch, yellow-white, fragrant flowers that bloom in late spring and early summer. This extraordinary specimen, one of the largest of its kind in California, is at the Huntington Botanical Gardens in San Marino.

Magnolia grandiflora.   PSM 22

BULL BAY, SOUTHERN MAGNOLIA.

One of the stateliest of American trees, the ever-green bull bay is native to the southeastern United States. It is noted for its glossy, leathery leaves, often with rusty-brown tomentum on their underside, and large, showy, fragrant white flowers up to a foot across that bloom from summer into early fall. The handsome flowers are followed by cone-like fruits in which conspicuous, crimson-pulped seeds are embedded. This impressive specimen, nearly 70 feet tall and with a spread of more than 50 feet, is in the southwest court of the Art Gallery at the Huntington Botanical Gardens in San Marino.

Macadamia integrifolia.   PSM 20

MACADAMIA NUT, QUEENSLAND NUT.

Named in honor of 19th-century physician John Macadam, the macadamia nut is a member of the protea family and native to Australia. It is grown commercially in Hawaii and, to a much lesser extent, in California for its famous, hard-shelled, sweet seed, considered by many to be the best-tasting of all nuts. Leaves are produced in whorls around the stem and white flowers occur in 100- to 300-flowered, 4- to 12-inch-long pendulous racemes. This remarkable specimen on the grounds of the Huntington Botanical Gardens in San Marino was one of the first of its kind introduced to California and, more than 30 feet tall with a spread of 20 feet, is one of the largest in the state.

Fragrant flowers of Delavay magnolia are yellow-white (below left).

The southern magnolia is famous for its fragrant, white flowers (above right).

The pink melaleuca has flowers in powder-puff-like heads and gnarled, twisted branches with thick, white, spongy bark.

PINK MELALEUCA, WESTERN TEA MYRTLE.

Melaleuca includes about 100 species of shrubs and trees native to Australia and the surrounding Pacific islands. It is named from the Greek words *melas,* meaning black, and *leukos,* meaning white. In their native habitat, the trunks are often scorched black by frequent brush fires but the limbs higher up on the tree remain white, hence the derivation of the botanical name.

The pink melaleuca, a member of the eucalyptus family and native to Australia, has gnarled, twisted branches with thick, white, spongy bark that sprawl along the ground in a picturesque manner similar to that of the Australian tea tree. Lavender or rose-pink flowers in powder-puff-like heads are produced sporadically throughout the year. This specimen, notable for its large, sprawling habit and curious bark, is on a bluff overlooking the ocean at Palisades Park in Santa Monica.

This dawn redwood at the Arboretum in Arcadia has foliage similar to the California redwood.

Metasequoia glyptostroboides. SGV 11
DAWN REDWOOD.

As its name implies, *Metasequoia* is related to *Sequoia,* the botanical name for the giant California redwoods. The Greek word *meta* means beyond and refers to the dawn redwood's ancestral relationship with *Sequoia.* Native to Szechwan province of China, the dawn redwood was first described from fossil material in 1941, while living plants were not brought to the attention of botanists until 1948. The dawn redwood existed hundreds of millions of years ago and, along with the ginkgo, cycads, and tree ferns, is considered a "living fossil." It is one of the few deciduous conifers; its leaves turn an attractive rusty-bronze before falling in late autumn. This magnificent planting near the Queen Anne Cottage at the Los Angeles State and County Arboretum in Arcadia contains specimens grown from the original lot of seeds distributed throughout the world in 1948.

NEW ZEALAND CHRISTMAS TREE.

Metrosideros is a group of trees and shrubs native from Australia to southern Africa, South America, and the islands of the Pacific. It is named from the Greek words *metra,* meaning middle, and *sideros,* meaning iron, referring to the hardness of the middle or heart-wood of the tree. Native to New Zealand, this member of the eucalyptus family attains peak bloom with lavish displays of dark red flowers in pincushion-like clusters in early summer, around December in the Southern Hemisphere, hence the common name. Equally arresting are swaying, pendulous masses — up to 8 feet long and 1 foot wide — of reddish-brown, hair-like aerial roots that drop from the branches, giving the tree a Medusan effect.

The New Zealand Christmas tree is an outstanding performer in humid coastal areas where growth of foliage and flowers and production of aerial roots are optimal. This remarkable specimen, on 4th Street near Adelaide Drive in Santa Monica, has an extraordinary number of aerial roots and is one of the largest and best formed trees of its kind in the area.

In Santa Monica, one of the most interesting New Zealand Christmas trees has swaying, pendulous masses of aerial roots and lavish, summer displays of red flowers.

An olive over 100 years old still produces shiny black fruit at Rancho San Pedro.

OLIVE.

Perhaps the most famous tree in the history of mankind, the olive has long been a symbol of peace and good-will. This grove of olives, more than 100 years old, is next to the Manuel Dominguez home, built in 1826 on Rancho San Pedro, first of the Spanish land grants given in the 1700s. Originally covering 76,000 acres, this grant stretched from present-day Hermosa Beach on the west, to Compton on the north, Long Beach on the east, and San Pedro and the Palos Verdes Peninsula on the south. The names of Dominguez, his heirs, and subsequent owners of Rancho San Pedro like Sepulveda, Carson, Watson, Del Amo, and Victoria are borne on many streets in the area.

The Battle of Dominguez Ranch occurred here on October 8 and 9, 1846, when Californians led by Jose Antonio Carillo, repelled U.S. forces under U.S.N. Capt. William Mervine in an attempt to recapture El Pueblo de Los Angeles. A plaque commemorates the battle and site, adjacent to the Dominguez home in present-day Compton, as a California Historical Landmark.

Oreopanax capitatus. S 4
OREOPANAX.

Oreopanax, a group of about 120 species of trees and shrubs native from Mexico to the West Indies and South America, is named from the Greek words *oreos,* meaning mountains, and *panakes,* meaning all-healing panacea. This name refers to the mountainous habitat of many of the species and their relationship to ginseng, widely used in many cultures for its medicinal value. This species is native to rain forests of the Atlantic slopes where, as a young plant, it is often found growing upon other plants. Rare in cultivation, it was first introduced to Southern California by Evans and Reeves Nursery in the 1930s. This planting of a half-dozen large trees is at 2959 Victoria Street in Compton.

Peltophorum dubium. PSM 23
PELTOPHORUM.
(Not Pictured)

Peltophorum, a group of about 15 species of trees or large shrubs native to South America, is named from the Greek words *pelta,* meaning a shield, and *phoreo,* meaning to bear. The name refers to the shield-shaped stigmas borne in the flowers. This member of the bean family is native to Brazil and Argentina, where it is commonly referred to as "ibira-pita." It has finely divided, fern-like foliage very similar to that of the jacaranda. Rare in California, it flowers only after a prolonged, hot summer and then is a spectacular sight because of its showy yellow flowers produced abundantly against the dark green foliage. These remarkable trees, the largest of their kind in California, are at the Huntington Botanical Gardens in San Marino.

The "Ganter Avocado" was planted in 1905 in Whittier.

A planting of large oreopanax trees with curious fruiting stalks is in Compton.

Persea americana. SE 9
AVOCADO, ALLIGATOR PEAR.

Persea, derived from a Greek name for an Egyptian tree, includes a group of trees native mainly to mountainous tropical areas of the New World. This avocado tree, in the parking lot of the Plymouth Congregational Church at 5800 Magnolia Avenue in Whittier, was planted in 1905. Originally a seedling from Mexico, it was one of the first avocados planted in Whittier, an area that played an important role in the growth of the avocado industry in Southern California. It is more than 60 feet tall, spreads 75 feet, and has a trunk 14 feet around.

Affectionately known as the "Ganter Avocado" in honor of one of its early owners, A.M. Ganter, it was a prolific bearer in its early years, producing as many as 6,000 fruits in a single season. In 1912, one of the owners, H.A. Woodworth, was able to sell a crop of 3,000 fruits from this tree for $6 a dozen and budwood from it for 22 cents a piece. Woodworth had the tree fenced to protect it from vandals and insured for

(Persea americana continued)

$30,000 against wind and fire by Lloyds of London. It is suitable for rootstock because of its disease resistance; seeds and budwood of the Ganter Avocado were distributed around the world from Israel to the Philippines, where offspring are still growing.

SAN MARINO   PSM 24

These trees are the remnants of the first commercial avocado grove in Southern California. Henry Huntington started the grove with seeds from avocados he had eaten at the Jonathan Club in Los Angeles. He planted them on his estate, now Huntington Botanical Gardens in San Marino, where they survive today at the northern end of the northwest side of the parking lot.

Persea americana 'Hass'.   SGV 31
HASS AVOCADO.

The Hass avocado, one of the most popular commercial varieties, had its beginning in the 1920s when Rudolf Hass, an early avocado grower, planted a number of seeds with the intention of using them as rootstock to which he could graft existing popular varieties. The graft on one particular seedling failed and when the seedling produced fruit several years later Hass recognized its superior qualities. This seedling tree, commemorated by a plaque from the California Historical Society, still stands at 426 West Road in La Habra Heights. It is the original Hass tree from which millions of genetically-identical offspring throughout the world are descended.

These avocados were planted by Henry E. Huntington.

The original Hass avocado still stands in La Habra Heights.

Canary Island date palms line a street in Elysian Park.

Phoenix canariensis.   C 17
CANARY ISLAND DATE PALM.

Phoenix, a group of palms native from Africa through the Middle East to Southeast Asia, is the Greek name for the date palm. Although related to the true date palm of commerce, the Canary Island date palm does not have edible fruit. About 100 years of age, this outstanding double-row planting, unsurpassed in number, age, and size of trees, lines Stadium Way between Academy Road and Scott Avenue in Elysian Park in Los Angeles. It is a remnant planting of the old Chavez Ravine Arboretum.

SANTA MONICA W 28

This parkway planting of Canary Island date palms, impressive in number and size of trees, lines Ocean Avenue in Santa Monica for nearly a mile along Palisades Park overlooking the Pacific Ocean.

Phoenix roebelenii. C 2

PYGMY DATE PALM.

Normally a single-headed palm known for its dwarf habit and graceful pinnate leaves, this extraordinary specimen has a phenomenal bushy crown composed of over 100 distinct but closely packed heads. It is on the grounds of the Doheny Campus of Mt. St. Mary's College, which includes many of the former estates once part of the exclusive 15-acre residential park known as Chester Place in the West Adams area of Los Angeles.

The Doheny Mansion, the "key" residence in Chester Place, was named for its most prominent owner, pioneer Los Angeles oilman and philanthropist E.L. Doheny. It is one of the best-preserved and most impressive Victorian residences remaining in the West Adams area.

This ombu, one of the few in California, has a striking, swollen, foot-like trunk to store water and white flowers in pendulous clusters.

Canary Island date palms beautify Santa Monica.

A multi-trunked pygmy date palm is a curious sight.

Phytolacca dioica. PSM 25

OMBU.

Phytolacca is named from the Greek word *phyton,* meaning a plant, and the Latin word *lacca,* referring to the lac insect from which a dark dye is extracted. The name refers to the staining qualities of the fruit of the ombu. This native of the expansive grasslands, called pampas, of southern South America is a curiosity noted for its gigantically swollen, foot-like trunk that serves as a water-storage organ in times of drought. Conspicuous as it dots the otherwise treeless pampas, the ombu is the unofficial national tree of Argentina and is prominent in its folklore. This notable specimen at the Huntington Botanical Gardens in San Marino, one of the few in Southern California, has a trunk more than 25 feet across at its base.

53

Canary Island pines make a fine planting in Whittier.

Pinus canariensis. SE 8

CANARY ISLAND PINE.

The pines are probably the most important and useful of the great group of cone-bearing plants called conifers. This particular species, native to the mountains of the Canary Islands in the Atlantic Ocean, provides one of the best-quality woods of all the pines. It is used for general construction and furniture and is tapped for resin. In the Canary Islands, the tee's needles are used for packing bananas for shipment. This exceptional *grande allée,* composed of nearly 200 trees unsurpassed in size, form, and esthetic quality, lines the 12000 block of Beverly Boulevard in Whittier.

The "Waldron Tree", the best known limber pine, is on Mt. Baden-Powell.

Pinus flexilis. SGV 34

LIMBER PINE.

This native of the Western United States is found in Southern California only above 8,000 feet elevation near the tops of the highest mountain peaks. Here, because of the extreme environmental conditions, the trees have an extraordinarily rugged, sculptured, and in some cases, a bonsaied appearance. Limber pines, the oldest living trees in Southern California, are close relatives of the world's oldest known living thing, the famous bristlecone pine, *P. longaeva,* which attains ages approaching 5,000 years.

The best known limber pine, locally called the "Waldron Tree," is along the trail on the north ridge at 9,300 feet elevation, just below the summit of Mt. Baden-Powell in Angeles National Forest, the second highest peak in Los Angeles County. Estimated to be a mere 2,000 years old, this weather-beaten, fantastically gnarled veteran, the exposed roots of which cling stubbornly to the exposed rocky ridge like the claws of a mountain lion, has withstood drought, hurricane-force winds, snow, ice, and sub-zero, arctic-like temperatures for centuries.

A large, well-shaped Italian stone pine is in Whittier.

Pinus pinea.   SE 15

ITALIAN STONE PINE.

Native to the northern Mediterranean region and the source of the pignolia nut of Southern Europe, the Italian stone pine is characterized by a wide-spreading, flat-topped crown. This exceptionally well-shaped tree at 7700 Painter Avenue in Whittier is an exemplary specimen of this typical form. More than 80 feet tall and with a trunk 16 feet around, it is one of the largest in Southern California.

This Torrey pine in Beverly Hills may be the largest of its kind.

Pinus torreyana.   W 1

TORREY PINE.

One of the rarest pines known, the Torrey pine is restricted in its native habitat to only two small areas along the Southern California coast. One is an area of coast bluffs just north of Del Mar near San Diego; the other, about 175 miles to the northwest, is on Santa Rosa Island in the Santa Barbara Channel. This magnificent specimen in Beverly Gardens Park near Beverly Drive and Santa Monica Boulevard in Beverly Hills may be the largest of its kind in the world. It stands more than 110 feet tall, spreads 75 feet, and has a trunk more than 20 feet around.

Pistacia atlantica.   SFV 9

MT. ATLAS PISTACHE.

Nearly 80 years old, these Mt. Atlas pistaches in western Antelope Valley still flower and fruit.

Pistacia, a group of about 10 species native to the Mediterranean region and northern Africa, is named from the Greek word for nut, *pistake.* These tremendous specimens, at Hunter Ranch near Three Points in western Antelope Valley, were planted about 1910 and are some of the largest and best-formed of their kind in California. Along with its close relative, *P. terebinthus,* Cyprus turpentine, the Mt. Atlas pistache has been used extensively in California for rootstock of *P. vera,* the edible pistachio nut of commerce.

Platanus racemosa.

WESTERN SYCAMORE, CALIFORNIA SYCAMORE.

Platanus, the Greek word for plane tree, is a group of deciduous trees native to Eurasia and North America. The only member native in California, the western or California sycamore occurs throughout the state primarily along watercourses. This splendid specimen, known locally as the "Eagle Tree" in honor of the great birds that once nested in its branches, formerly marked the northern boundary of Rancho San Pedro and has been a natural landmark for 200 years. Still standing on an easement between apartments at the corner of Short and Poppy Avenues in Compton, it has a trunk 21 feet around, spreads 50 feet, and is 70 feet tall.

This California sycamore is known as the "Eagle Tree" in honor of the great birds that once nested in its branches.

In Polynesia fragrant plumeria flowers are highly esteemed and widely used for personal adornment.

Plumeria rubra.

PLUMERIA, FRANGIPANI.

Plumeria, a group of about 8 species of shrubs or small trees native to the American tropics, is named in honor of Charles Plumier, 17th-century French botanist, traveler, and author. Native to Mexico and Central America, the frangipani is one of the most widely cultivated plants throughout the tropical regions of the world. In Polynesia, especially, it is highly esteemed for its handsome, fragrant flowers, widely used for personal adornment. It is the most common flower of Hawaiian leis. Uncommon in California, this outstanding, red-flowered specimen on Davidson Drive near the corner of Norwalk Boulevard and Beverly Drive in Whittier is one of the largest in the state. At 20 feet tall, it rivals even the largest plumerias in the tropics.

Populus fremontii.
WESTERN COTTONWOOD.

Populus is a group of about 35 species of deciduous trees native to northern temperate zones. It was probably a species of *Populus* that was referred to in Psalms 137:2 as a willow upon which Israeli captives in Babylon hung their harps and wept.

Located in an onion field on 45th Street East at Avenue K near Lancaster in the Antelope Valley, this remarkable specimen is visible for miles in the wide-open expanses of the Mojave Desert. This well-shaped tree is nearly 90 feet tall, spreads 70 feet, and has a trunk more than 16 feet around.

The largest western cottonwood is in the Antelope Valley.

Pseudobombax flowers when leafless in February at the Arboretum in Arcadia.

Pseudobombax grandiflorum.
PSEUDOBOMBAX.

Pseudobombax is similar to and a close relative of the true *Bombax,* hence the prefix *pseudo* in the name. *Bombax* is named from the Greek word *bombyx,* meaning silk, referring to the fluffy, silky hairs in which the seeds are embedded in the seed capsules. Native to Brazil, this impressive tree is a rare find because of its tropical nature. Located at the Los Angeles State and County Arboretum in Arcadia, the institution responsible for introducing it and other flowering trees of merit to Southern California, it is the largest of its kind in the state. Although it has handsome, palmately compound leaves, it is most arresting in the dead of winter when, devoid of foliage, striking, white, shaving-brush-like flowers burst from black, bullet-shaped buds at the ends of bare branches.

Pseudotsuga macrocarpa.
BIG-CONE SPRUCE.

Pseudotsuga is named from the Greek words *pseudo,* meaning false, and *tsuga,* a Japanese name for hemlock. This native of Southern California and Baja California is a relative of the better-known Douglas fir, *Pseudotsuga menziesii.* In actuality, it is neither a fir nor, as the common name implies, a spruce. This extraordinary specimen is growing in Angeles National Forest below Mt. San Antonio, or Old Baldy, which at 10,064 feet is the highest mountain in Los Angeles County. This big-cone spruce is the national champion of its species and appears in the *National Register of Big Trees,* published by the American Forestry Association. It is more than 130 feet tall, spreads 85 feet, and has a trunk nearly 24 feet around.

This national champion big-cone spruce grows on Mt. San Antonio, the highest peak in Los Angeles County.

57

Quercus engelmannii.   PSM 27

MESA OAK, ENGELMANN OAK.

Reported to be the largest specimen of its kind in Southern California, this magnificent tree, a native of the area, is south of the library at the Huntington Botanical Gardens in San Marino. The tree is 45 feet tall, has a trunk 10 feet around, and is unsurpassed for the beauty of its symmetrical, 80-foot, umbrella-shaped crown.

ARCADIA   SGV 13

This native colony of mesa oaks at the Los Angeles State and County Arboretum in Arcadia comprises the last remaining intact stand of mesa oak woodland in the world. It appears much as one would have found it 300 years ago. Once widespread from Los Angeles to San Diego, the mesa oak has been largely depleted by urbanization and exists, for the most part, as scattered individuals in its range.

An outstanding mesa oak is at the Huntington Botanical Gardens.

The Arboretum in Arcadia contains a native stand of mesa oaks.

The rare Indian oak has the undersides of the leaves clothed in a pure white, felt-like material.

Quercus leucotricuphora.   SGV 14

INDIAN OAK.

This handsome, evergreen oak has leaves notable for their dark green uppersides and undersides clothed with a pure white, close felt-like material. The young shoots and new growth are clothed in a similar manner. Native to the Himalayas up to 8,000 feet elevation, it is always found growing with a tree rhododendron. Its acorns are eaten by pigeons, bears, and the large langur, a type of monkey.

This magnificent specimen, the most beautiful and largest of its kind in Southern California, is at the Los Angeles State and County Arboretum in Arcadia.

Quercus lobata.   SFV 12

VALLEY OAK, WHITE OAK.

A deciduous tree, the valley oak is California's most noble oak. This outstanding specimen is in Liberty Canyon in Malibu Creek State Park in the Santa Monica Mountains southwest of Agoura Hills. More than 60 feet tall, with a spread of 75 feet, and a trunk nearly 17 feet around, it is the largest in the area and is known locally as the "Alpha Oak" because of its stature. The tree is in excellent condition and has survived many fires, the latest in 1982.

Malibu Creek State Park contains the southernmost valley oak savanna in California and one of the few protected bottomland valley oak savannas anywhere in the state. Father Crespi, who was with the Portola Expedition that was exploring California in 1770, noted in his diary in April of that year that the oaks of this area of the San Fernando Valley were the most magnificent of any he had encountered in all of his travels. The area around the "Alpha Oak" has been designated a state nature preserve to permit reproduction to restock this prime habitat. (Not Pictured)

CANOGA PARK   SFV 6

Located at Orcutt Ranch Horticulture Center in the Canoga Park area of Los Angeles in the San Fernando Valley oak tree, this extraordinary valley oak is 70 feet tall, has a trunk 18 feet around, and spreads nearly 125 feet. It is a remnant of once-extensive oak savannas that covered much of the San Fernando Valley but with few exceptions, such as the Chatsworth Reservoir oaks, have been destroyed.

A stately English oak grows at the Huntington botanical Gardens.

Two, well-formed cork oaks in Rosemead have very thick, deeply furrowed, spongy bark.

This valley oak at Orcutt Ranch Horticulture Center is a remnant of once-extensive oak savannas.

Quercus robur.   PSM 28
ENGLISH OAK.

These two magnificent specimens, the largest of their kind in Southern California, are in a magnificent setting on the lawn south of the library at the Huntington Botanical Gardens in San Marino.

Once widespread in vast groves throughout Europe, eastern Asia, and northern Africa but now less common, this oak is the most important tree in English history. It is said that the famous round table — some 18 feet in diameter — around which King Arthur and his knights held court was cut from the trunk of an English oak. King Henry VIII always delighted in showing the table to visiting royalty. The traditional yule log from which the Christmas fire was kindled was of English oak. Anyone unfortunate enough to have been found guilty of cutting down this oak in England in the 7th century was fined 30 shillings, but if the tree was large enough for 30 hogs to stand in its shadow, the fine was 60 shillings.

The wood of these trees was preferred above all others for ship-building because of its many admirable qualities. It is hard, strong, tough, durable but tolerably flexible and not too heavy or readily penetrated by water. If struck by a cannon ball, it did not splinter, enabling the hole to be plugged easily. When British sailors sang, "Hearts of oaks are our ships, Gallant tars are our men . . .," they knew that as long as these oaks were plentiful in the British Isles, British ships manned by British men willing to die for the crown would be sailing the seven seas.

Quercus suber.   SGV 2
CORK OAK.

The very thick, spongy bark of this species native to the Mediterranean region furnishes the cork of commerce. These two large, well-formed specimens are on Mission Drive near Willard Avenue in Rosemead.

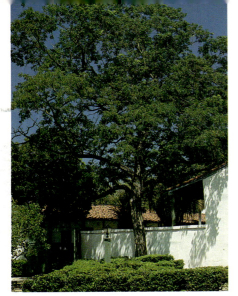

These 140-year-old black locust trees still produce clusters of fragrant, white flowers in spring.

Robinia pseudoacacia. S 3

BLACK LOCUST.

Robinia is named in honor of Jean Robin, professor of botany at Leipzig University, and his son, Vespasien, both herbalists in the 16th and 17th centuries to French royalty. The Robins introduced the first locust trees to Europe. The black locust, a deciduous member of the bean family and native of the Eastern and Central United States, is noted for its handsome, pinnately-compound leaves and dense clusters, up to 10 inches long, of fragrant white flowers that appear in spring on nearly bare branches. These notable trees, planted about 1850 by Jonathan Temple around his ranch house at Rancho Los Cerritos in present-day Long Beach, are the first of their kind introduced to California.

Schinus molle. SE 19

CALIFORNIA PEPPER TREE.

Schinus is derived from the Greek word *schinos,* the name for the mastic tree to which it is related and resembles in its resinous exudate. This relative of the cashew, mango, and poison oak is actually native to Peru but has become so well established in California that, like the eucalypts, it is considered almost a native species. This large, well-formed specimen is near the mansion at Neff Park in La Mirada, formerly Windermere Ranch owned by Andrew McNally of Rand McNally atlas fame. Planted by McNally in the late 1800s, it now is 45 feet tall, spreads over 75 feet, and has a trunk over 12 feet around.

A large, well-formed California pepper tree in La Mirada has fern-like foliage and scarlet berries.

The crown-of-gold tree, our best yellow-flowering tree, is a spectacular sight in late summer.

Senna spectabilis var. *spectabilis.* C 6

CROWN-OF-GOLD TREE.

Senna is the Greek name for a group of trees and shrubs providing senna, an important compound in pharmacy. Closely related to cassias and, in fact, once included in that group, this tropical tree is a relatively recent introduction and is still uncommon in Southern California. This outstanding specimen, the largest of its kind in the state, is at the back entrance to the County Hall of Administration in downtown Los Angeles. It is a spectacular sight in late summer with its profuse upright masses of yellow flowers capping the circular crown of dark green, pinnate leaves.

This relatively young redwood was planted in 1923 by General John J. Pershing in South Pasadena.

COAST REDWOOD.

Sequoia was named in honor of the 19th-century Cherokee, Sequoyah, inventor of the Cherokee alphabet. Although this specimen in front of the War Memorial Building at 435 Fair Oaks Avenue in South Pasadena cannot begin to compare with its 300-foot-tall sisters in Northern California, it is still exceptional in its own right. It was planted by General John J. Pershing on July 31, 1923 and is marked by a plaque commemorating this event.

Spathodea campanulata.   W 37

AFRICAN TULIP TREE.

Cup-shaped, bright orange flowers crown this African tulip-tree during summer in west Los Angeles.

Spathodea, a small group of trees native to Tropical Africa, is named from the Greek words *spathe,* an urn-like or cup-like structure surrounding certain flowers, and *odes,* meaning similar, referring to the flowers of this tree that resemble a spathe. Nearly 40 feet tall with a trunk 6 feet around, this specimen, essentially a tropical species and rare in California, is the largest of its kind in the state. Located at 11927 Venice Boulevard in west Los Angeles, it is a special sight in summer and early fall when its crown is covered with 3-inch, cup-shaped, bright orange flowers.

The African tulip tree has spread and naturalized to many tropical areas around the world. In wet areas, the clusters of flowers collect rain and the unopened flower buds lie under water almost until opening. Unopened buds contain ill-smelling and ill-tasting water that squirts out when buds are pinched or squeezed, making excellent water pistols for children. Along the Gold Coast of Africa the tree is known as the ''baton de sorcier'' because the flowers are used in black magic and the wood for drums by witch doctors.

Exotic flowers mark this giant bird-of-paradise.

Strelitzia nicolai.   C 4

GIANT BIRD-OF-PARADISE.

The name *Strelitzia* honors Charlotte Sophia, Duchess of Mecklenberg-Strelitz, who became queen to King George III of England in the late 1700s. Grown primarily for its dramatic display of large banana-like leaves, the giant bird-of-paradise with its tree-like multiple trunks is a close relative of the trunkless, shrubby bird-of-paradise, *S. reginae,* the official flower of Los Angeles. This tremendous specimen on the west side of Orthopaedic Hospital in the 2400 block of Flower Street in Los Angeles is unsurpassed for number and size of trunks and esthetic features of leaves and flowers.

Golden yellow flowers are the trademark of this golden trumpet tree, introduced in 1964 by the Arboretum in Arcadia.

Tabebuia chrysotricha. SGV 15
GOLDEN TRUMPET TREE.

Tabebuia, a group of about 100 species of large or small trees related to the jacaranda, is derived from the South American Indian name for these trees, *tacyba bebuya.* The tree is notable for its bright golden yellow, trumpet-like flowers borne in showy clusters from March to April. Because of its airy and open crown providing excellent-quality shade and recognized pest and disease resistance, these trees are well adapted to various uses in the home garden and landscape. These remarkable specimens at the Los Angeles State and County Arboretum in Arcadia were first introduced by the Arboretum in 1964.

Another Arboretum introduction, this ipe with pink flowers is the largest in California.

Tabebuia impetiginosa. SGV 16
IPE, PINK TABEBUIA.

Native to Argentina and Brazil, where it is called "lapacho negro," ipe is just one of several outstanding flowering trees to grace the Southern California landscape which have been introduced by the Los Angeles State and County Arboretum in Arcadia. This splendid specimen, the largest and most beautiful of its kind in California, is near the gift shop on the Arboretum grounds. First introduced in 1964, it is a spectacular sight in spring when its bare branches are heavily laden with masses of pink-to-lavender, yellow-throated, tubular flowers.

Taiwania cryptomeroides. PSM 29
TAIWANIA.

A group of two species of evergreen trees native to Taiwan (from which the name is derived) and Yunnan Province of China, *Taiwania* is one of the tallest of Old World conifers, attaining heights up to 200 feet with trunks 30 feet around. This relative of the California redwoods is virtually unknown outside of its native habitat, where it was once common but now is rare. Located in the Huntington Botanical Gardens in San Marino, it is the largest and finest specimen of its kind in the United States.

This taiwania at the Huntington Botanical Gardens is a relative of the California redwoods and virtually unknown outside its native habitat.

TALAUMA.

Talauma is a derivative of a colloquial name used for this group of trees by natives in Central and South America. This particular species, native to the Himalayas, was introduced by Evans and Reeves Nursery in the 1930s but is still rare in the landscape. A close relative of the magnolias, it is noted for its evergreen habit, its tropical-looking leaves up to 20 inches long and 4 inches wide, and its creamy white magnolia-like flowers. This outstanding specimen, one of the largest and finest in the state, is in a courtyard of an apartment complex at 1524 Yale Street in Santa Monica.

Talauma has magnolia-like flowers and big, tropical-looking leaves.

The bald cypress is a deciduous tree with a striking late-fall display of rusty-brown foliage.

Taxodium distichum var. *nutans.*   C19

BALD CYPRESS.

Taxodium, two species of trees related to the California redwoods and native to the southern United States and Mexico, derives its name from the Greek words *taxus,* the name for yews, and *odes,* meaning resembles, referring to the superficial similarities of these two groups of conifers. This extraordinary specimen is in a lawn planting and is a remnant of the old Chavez Ravine Arboretum in Elysian Park in Los Angeles. The tree is outstanding in its columnar form and its deciduous habit that results in a striking late-fall display of bright orange to rusty-brown foliage.

Native to swamps and streamsides in the southeastern United States, the bald cypress is Florida's longest-living tree. It is noted for its peculiar knee-like projections, called pneumatophores, rising from submerged roots and protruding above the water. It is thought that these unusual formations supply oxygen and anchorage for the roots in boggy, swampy habitats. Surprisingly, seeds of the bald cypress cannot germinate in water although in nature trees need large amounts of water to survive. Apparently, seeds germinate during the infrequent droughts when the swamps and streams become dry. Once germinated and grown into seedlings, they are able to tolerate mud and standing water.

Taxodium mucronatum. SE 14

MONTEZUMA CYPRESS.

Called "ahuehueta" meaning old man of water, the Montezuma cypress is one of the best-known trees of Mexico. A tree at Santa Maria del Tule in Oaxaca has a trunk 160 feet around and is said to be several thousand years old. An unfounded legend states that the great explorer Alexander von Humboldt carved his initials in this tree. The Spaniard Cortez is said to have wept under another Montezuma cypress, the "Arbol de la Noche Triste," in Popotla during his retreat from the Aztecs in 1520. Cortez stopped to rest under this tree and wept upon contemplating his fate and that of his troops who were slain by the Aztecs.

Evergreen in the mild Southern California coastal climates, the Montezuma cypress is noted for its handsome weeping habit and fine-textured leaves. More than 80 feet tall, spreading 60 feet, and with a trunk nearly 13 feet around, this graceful specimen in Kennedy Park at 8600 Painter Avenue in Whittier is one of the largest of its kind in California. Well suited for large lawns and park areas, the Montezuma cypress is worthy of wider cultivation.

SAN MARINO PSM 30

This grove of Montezuma cypress in the Huntington Botanical Gardens in San Marino is unsurpassed in size, number of trees, weeping habit, and landscape setting.

A large Montezuma cypress (right) is in Whittier while another of the same kind (below) is in an unsurpassed setting at the Huntington Botanical Gardens.

This large silver linden is well adapted to drought, heat, and smog, has handsome foliage.

Tilia tomentosa. SGV 17

SILVER LINDEN.

In Greek mythology, Zeus, god of the heavens, and Hermes, god of communication, commerce, thievery, eloquence, and research and science, at one time visited earth disguised as humans. Turned away by all others when seeking shelter for the evening, they were finally taken in by Philemon and Baucis, husband and wife of a humble home. So pleased were Zeus and Hermes that they revealed their identity and granted Philemon and Baucis one wish. The husband and wife wished that one would not survive the other. Their wish was granted when, later, near the end of their lives, they were happily transformed into linden trees by the gods and their house became a magnificent temple, outside of which they stood. *Tilia,* a group of about 30 species of trees native to the northern temperate zone, is also the Latin word for these trees.

This particular species, native to southeastern Europe, is the most beautiful of the lindens. Its two-colored leaves, green on the upper surface and silvery-white below, are a striking sight when the wind moves them, rippling the crown of foliage into a storyland of green and silver. The best linden for Southern California, it is well adapted to drought, heat, and smog. This remarkable specimen at the Los Angeles State and County Arboretum in Arcadia is unsurpassed for size, form, and beauty.

Wood of the linden is white, soft, free of knots, and light, making it preferred above all others by woodcarvers. It has been used for toys, panels, and woodenware. Many of the fine carvings in Windsor Castle and at the Duke of Devenshire's mansion are of linden wood. One of Europe's most popular trees, it has long been favored for parks, avenues, and streets. Many streets and even cities are known for their lindens.

A 100-year-old tipu tree in Elysian Park produces yellow flowers throughout the summer.

Tipuana tipu.   C 20

TIPU TREE.

Tipuana is a derivative of a South American Indian name for this attractive tree. Native to southern Brazil and Argentina, where it is called "tipa blanca" and is used in general light carpentry, the tipu tree is noted for its broadly spreading crown of handsome, pinnate leaves and golden yellow flowers produced throughout the summer. This outstanding specimen, a remnant of the old Chavez Ravine Arboretum in Elysian Park in Los Angeles, is the largest of its kind in California. It is 70 feet tall, spreads over 100 feet, and has four main trunks, each 7 feet around.

BEL-AIR   W 18

This impressive tipu tree on the south side of the Hotel Bel-Air in the Bel-Air area of Los Angeles is noted for its outstanding umbrella-shaped crown and branch structure that is best viewed by standing directly beneath the tree. In midsummer, masses of fallen yellow-orange flowers carpet the street beneath the tree.

BRENTWOOD   W 20

Located at a private residence at 685 Elkins Road in the Brentwood area of Los Angeles, this magnificent tipu tree is unsurpassed for its symmetrical, spreading branches radiating from the trunk like spokes of a wheel to support its broad crown.

LOS ANGELES   W 9

These two well-formed tipu trees with their large, densely-foliaged, bowl-shaped crowns are located on the grounds of the Los Angeles Country Club at 10101 Wilshire Boulevard in Los Angeles.

An impressively shaped tipu tree is at the Hotel Bel-Air.

Tipu trees in Brentwood (above) and Los Angeles (below).

A large multi-trunked California bay is at California State Polytechnic University in Pomona.

Umbellularia californica.   SGV 29
CALIFORNIA BAY.

Umbellularia is named from the Latin word *umbella*, referring to the flowerstalks being in a cluster and all radiating from a single point, a floral structure called an umbel. This handsome, native California tree is noted for its checkered, deeply-fissured, dark gray bark and laurel-like leaves which when crushed release a strongly aromatic odor not too unlike that of leaves of the European bay tree, a close relative. In fact, the leaves can be used judiciously in the kitchen as a substitute for true bay leaves.

This multi-branched specimen behind Los Olivos Commons on the campus of California State Polytechnic University in Pomona is more than 80 feet tall, spreads 60 feet, and has a trunk 14 feet around. Its tall, upright habit is more typical of California bay trees found in forested situations in contrast to bushy types in exposed locations.

Vitis vinifera.   SGV 3
GRAPE.

Vitis is the Latin name for the wine or vineyard grape of the Old World. Most references define a tree as a woody plant under which one is able to walk. Although stretching this definition slightly, this grape vine is woody and, supported by an arbor, one can walk beneath it; hence, it is included here. More importantly, this vine, protected and honored in Grapevine Park on Mission Drive in San Gabriel, is a remnant of the first vineyard established by the Spanish padres, adjacent to their mission, in the early 19th-century.

The San Gabriel Mission grew to be known as the "Queen of Missions" in California and was the crown jewel of the chain of missions established throughout the state by the Spanish government in its efforts to colonize and bring Christianity to the area. The missions played an important role in the introduction of exotic plants into California. In fact, their nurseries were the only source of plants for the early settlers. The Spanish padres introduced the first lemons, limes, oranges, figs, olives, pecans, dates, apples, pears, pomegranates, plums, grapes, and bananas to California, in addition to many ornamentals and other flowering plants including the California pepper tree from South America.

This 150-year-old grape is next to the San Gabriel Mission.

Washingtonia filifera.   SGV 20
CALIFORNIA FAN PALM.

Washingtonia, two species of fan palms native to Baja California and the deserts of Arizona and California, honors George Washington, first president of the United States. This remarkable planting consisting of more than 200 large, mature specimens in a double *grande allée,* is the largest grouping of these trees outside their native habitat. It is the only species of palm native to California, where it is found naturally in the desert canyons and washes of Southern and Baja California. This planting lines both entrance roads to Monrovia Nursery on Foothill Boulevard in Azusa.

LOS ANGELES   C 1

Exceeded in number only by the above-mentioned planting in Azusa, this impressive grove of California fan palms is on the grounds of Rosedale Cemetery at 1800 Washington Boulevard in Los Angeles. These palms are more than 100 years old and are some of the largest of their kind in cultivation.

SAN MARINO   PSM 31

These two magnificent California fan palms behind a private residence at 1544 Cambridge Road in San Marino were removed as seedlings from a native stand in a desert canyon near present-day Palm Springs by a mining prospector named Stockton. He transported them by burro to their present location and planted them sometime in the 1840s near a stream that provided water for the San Gabriel Mission. Later, in the early 1900s, a station on the Pacific Electric Railway was built adjacent to the two trees and called Palms in recognition of the two landmarks. This railway built by Henry Huntington was an interurban network of the famous "Big Red Cars" and once served all of greater Los Angeles from the mountains to the sea. The twin trees were commemorated as historic landmarks in 1941 by the San Marino Garden Club with a bronze plaque, still in place today.

An exceptional planting of California fan palms is in Azusa.

San Marino is home to these two California fan palms.

Another large group of California fan palms is in Los Angeles.

The tallest Mexican fan palms are at the Arboretum in Arcadia.

A most unusual Mexican fan palm is in Pasadena.

Washingtonia robusta.   SGV 18
MEXICAN FAN PALM.

Taller and more slender than its close relative, the California fan palm, the Mexican fan palm is the most conspicuous tree on the Los Angeles skyline. Emblematic of a unique lifestyle and captured in numerous advertisements, magazines, books, and promotional media, the Mexican fan palm is the tree most associated with Southern California, although it occurs naturally only in Baja California. During the land booms of the late 1800s and early 1900s, thousands of these palms were used to line roads of new subdivisions, farms, and ranches. Many of these first plantings survive today. This grove of outstanding specimens, about 100 years old and some 100 feet tall, was planted in the 1880s by E.J. "Lucky" Baldwin on his estate, Rancho Santa Anita. Today, these trees encircle the lagoon in the Historic Area of the Los Angeles State and County Arboretum in Arcadia.

PASADENA   PSM 7

This single Mexican fan palm at 399 Ninita Parkway in Pasadena had a difficult time deciding which way was up. It is exceptional because of its up, down, and back-up-again serpentine trunk.

SANTA MONICA   W 29

This grove of Mexican fan palms is notable due to the graceful curving habit of its trees and its unique setting along the promenade on top of the bluff overlooking the Pacific Ocean in Palisades Park in Santa Monica.

Santa Monica is home to these graceful Mexican fan palms.

GEOGRAPHICAL LISTINGS

OF THE EXCEPTIONAL TREES.

To facilitate locating and viewing the trees, this book divides Los Angeles County into seven geographical regions. For each region the trees which occur there are listed and numbered. The number of each tree corresponds to a number on the accompanying map of each region denoting the tree's location. Within each geographical region, the trees have been placed in sequential order depending on their location.

Maps provided by:
Perry Supply Co., Inc./MAPS, etc., Canoga Park, CA

PASADENA-SAN MARINO PSM
Map, page 76

1. Angophora costata
2. Angophora costata
3. Cedrus deodara
4. Chorisia speciosa
5. Ficus macrophylla
6. Cinnamomum camphora
7. Washingtonia robusta
8. Brahea edulis
9. Castanospermum australe
10. Cedrus atlantica 'Glauca'
11. Chionanthus retusus
12. Chorisia insignis
13. Cupressus cashmeriana
14. Cupressus guadalupensis
15. Dombeya cacuminum
16. Ficus macrophylla
17. Ficus thonningii
18. Keteleeria davidiana
19. Livistona decipiens
20. Macadamia integrifolia
21. Magnolia delavayi
22. Magnolia grandiflora
23. Peltophorum dubium
24. Persea americana
25. Phytolacca dioica
26. Pterocarya stenoptera
27. Quercus engelmannii
28. Quercus robur
29. Taiwania cryptomerioides
30. Taxodium mucronatum
31. Washingtonia filifera
32. Jacaranda mimosifolia
33. Eucalyptus citriodora
34. Sequoia sempervirens

SAN GABRIEL VALLEY SGV
Map, page 77

1. Liquidambar styraciflua
2. Quercus suber
3. Vitis vinifera
4. Quercus agrifolia
5. Chorisia speciosa
6. Enterolobium contortisiliquum
7. Erythrina falcata
8. Eucalyptus globulus
9. Ficus sycomorus
10. Juglans nigra
11. Metasequoia glyptostroboides
12. Pseudobombax grandiflora
13. Quercus engelmannii
14. Quercus leucotricophora
15. Tabebuia chrysotricha
16. Tabebuia impetiginosa
17. Tilia tomentosa
18. Washingtonia robusta
19. Calodendrum capense
20. Washingtonia filifera
21. Ficus macrophylla
22. Araucaria cunninghamiana
23. Cedrus deodara
24. Cedrus deodara
25. Ficus elastica 'Decora'
26. Brachychiton discolor
27. Ginkgo biloba
28. Cinnamomum camphora
29. Umbellularia californica
30. Eucalyptus citriodora
31. Persea americana 'Hass'
32. Pseudotsuga macrocarpa
33. Quercus chrysolepis
34. Pinus flexilis

SOUTHEAST SE
Map, page 72

1. Acrocarpus fraxinifolius
2. Araucaria bidwillii
3. Casimiroa edulis
4. Ficus macrophylla
5. Liriodendron tulipifera
6. Plumeria rubra
7. Bischofia javanica
8. Pinus canariensis
9. Persea americana
10. Cedrus libani
11. Grevillea robusta
12. Ficus benghalensis
13. Juglans 'Paradoxa'
14. Taxodium mucronatum
15. Pinus pinea
16. Bauhinia variegata
17. Jacaranda mimosifolia
18. Brachychiton acerifolius
19. Schinus molle

CENTRAL C
Map, page 73

1. Washingtonia filifera
2. Phoenix roebelenii
3. Ficus macrophylla
4. Strelitzia nicolai
5. Citrus x paradisi
6. Senna spectabilis var. spectabilis
7. Ficus macrophylla
8. Erythrina crista-galli
9. Agathis robusta
10. Baphia chrysophylla
11. Brachychiton populneus
12. Calodendrum capense
13. Cedrela toona
14. Cryptocarya rubra
15. Dalbergia sissoo
16. Ficus religiosa
17. Phoenix canariensis
18. Quercus cerris
19. Taxodium distichum var. nutans
20. Tipuana tipu
21. Erythrina falcata

SOUTHERN S
Map, page 74

1. Ficus macrophylla
2. Cupressus sempervirens
3. Robinia pseudoacacia
4. Oreopanax capitatus
5. Olea europaea
6. Platanus racemosa
7. Eucalyptus tereticornis
8. Eucalyptus ficifolia
9. Ficus macrophylla

SAN FERNANDO VALLEY SFV
Map, page 75

1. Quercus agrifolia
2. Quercus agrifolia
3. Carya illinoensis
4. Eucalyptus globulus
5. Quercus agrifolia
6. Quercus lobata
7. Quercus agrifolia
8. Populus fremontii
9. Pistacia atlantica
10. Acer macrophyllum
11. Fraxinus velutina var. coriacea
12. Quercus lobata

WESTSIDE W
Map, page 78

1. Pinus torreyana
2. Lagunaria patersonii
3. Ficus retusa
4. Cinnamomum camphora
5. Lophostemon conferta
6. Archontophoenix cunninghamiana
7. Chiranthodendron pentadactylon
8. Ficus macrophylla
9. Tipuana tipu
10. Casuarina cunninghamiana
11. Eucalyptus deglupta
12. Eucalyptus grandis
13. Ficus rubiginosa
14. Harpullia pendula
15. Kigelia pinnata
16. Chorisia speciosa
17. Lonchocarpus nitidus
18. Tipuana tipu
19. Araucaria heterophylla
20. Tipuana tipu
21. Erythrina speciosa
22. Dioon spinulosum
23. Ficus macrophylla
24. Metrosideros excelsus
25. Eucalyptus diversicolor
26. Leptospermum laevigatum
27. Melaleuca nesophila
28. Phoenix canariensis
29. Washingtonia robusta
30. Ficus macrophylla
31. Erythrina caffra
32. Ficus macrophylla
33. Eucalyptus deanei
34. Talauma hodgsonii
35. Eucalyptus amplifolia
36. Ficus macrophylla
37. Spathodea campanulata
38. Erythrina abyssinica

Location Map for Trees in the
SOUTHEAST Region   Code: SE

See page 71 for complete listings

Location Map for Trees in the
CENTRAL Region   Code: C

See page 71 for complete listings

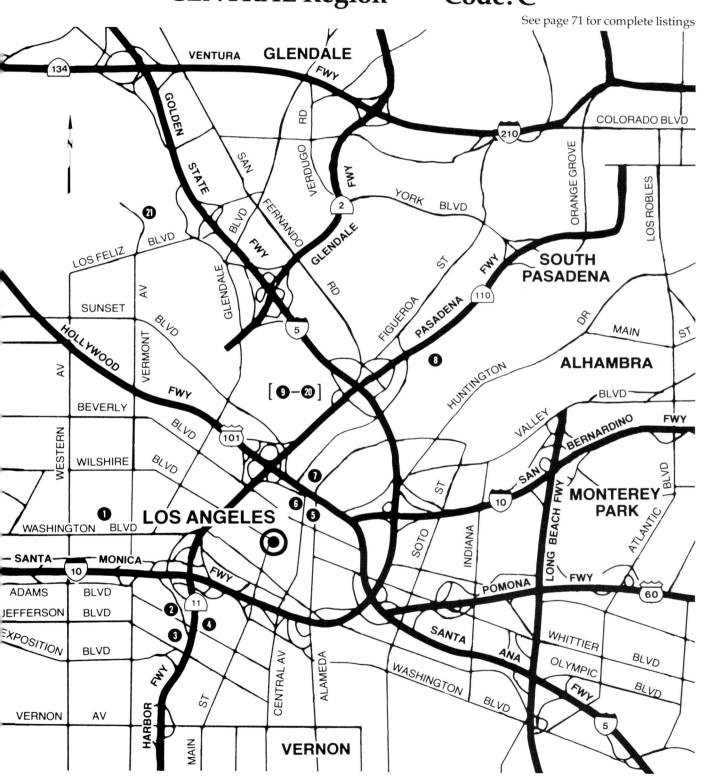

Location Map for Trees in the
SOUTHERN Region   Code: S

See page 71 for complete listing

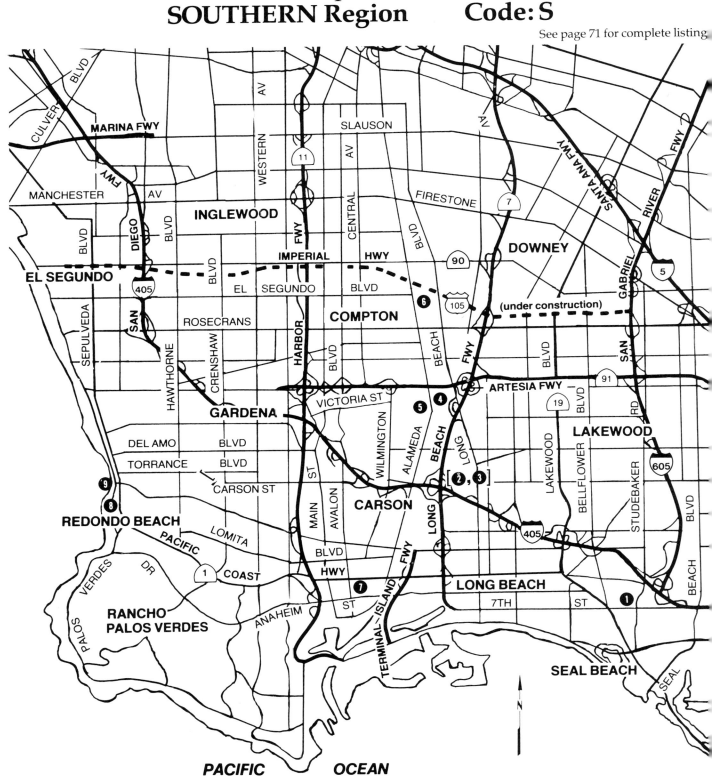

Location Map for Trees in the
SAN FERNANDO VALLEY Region

Code: SFV

See page 71 for complete listings

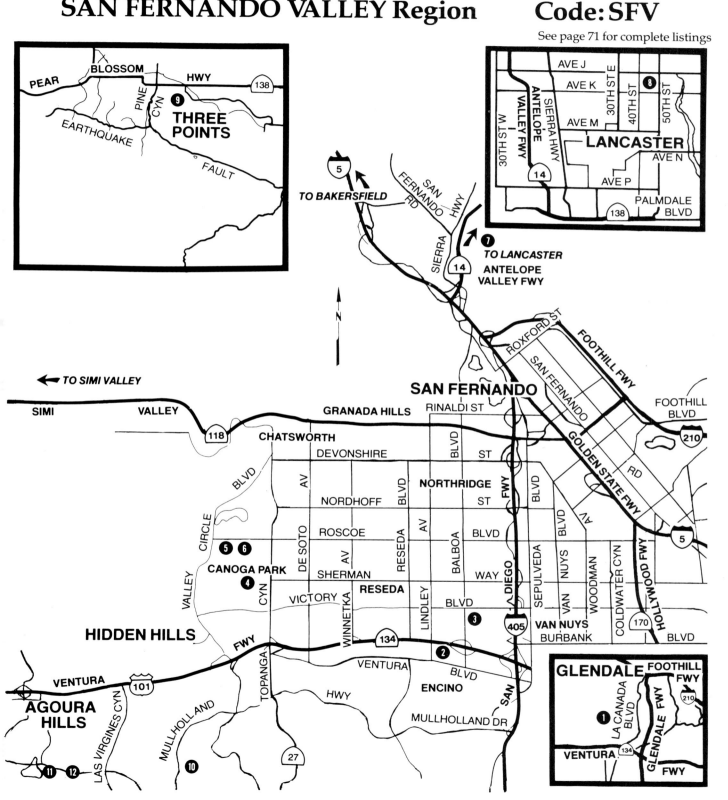

Location Map for Trees in the
PASADENA-SAN MARINO Region

Code: PSM

See page 71 for complete listings

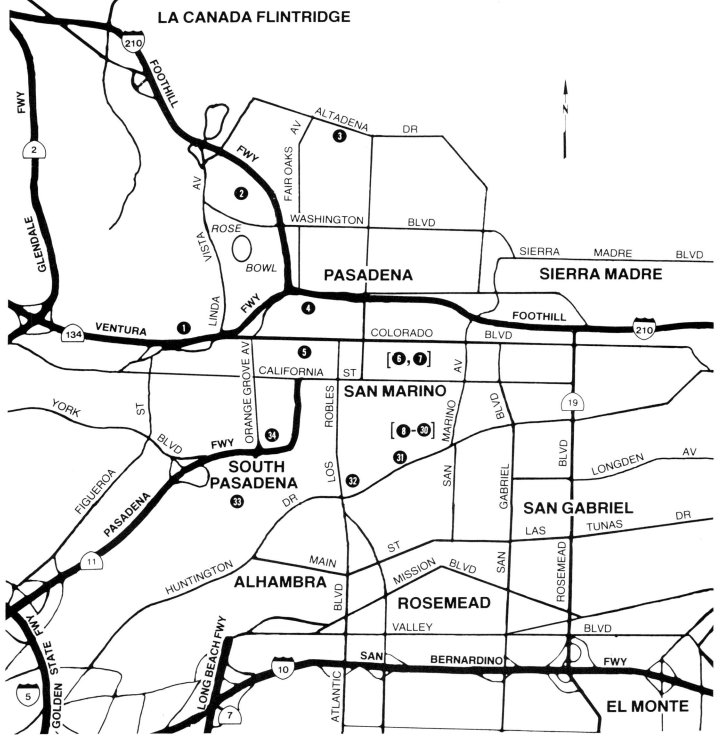

Location Map for Trees in the
SAN GABRIEL VALLEY Region   Code: SGV

See page 71 for complete listings

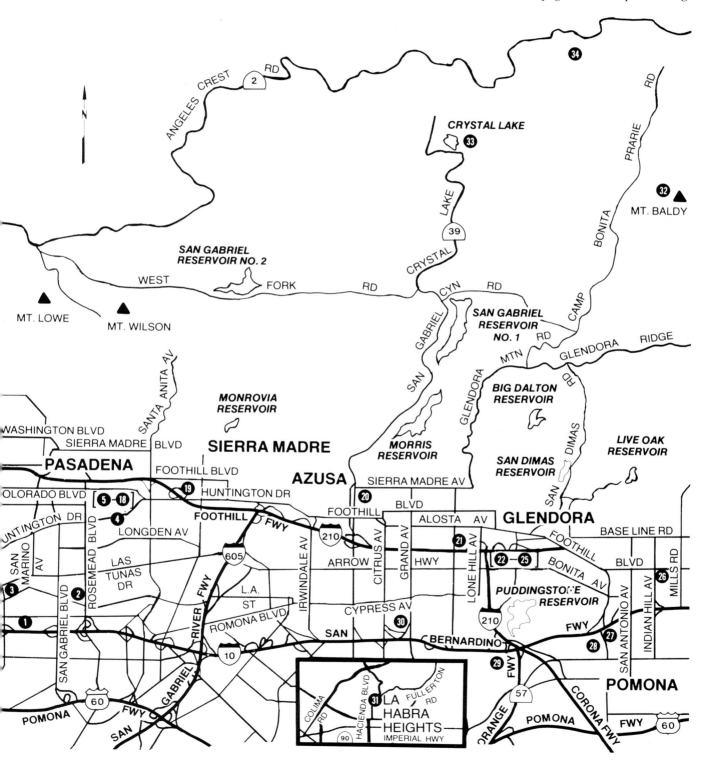

Location Map for Trees in the
WESTSIDE Region   Code: W

See page 71 for complete listin

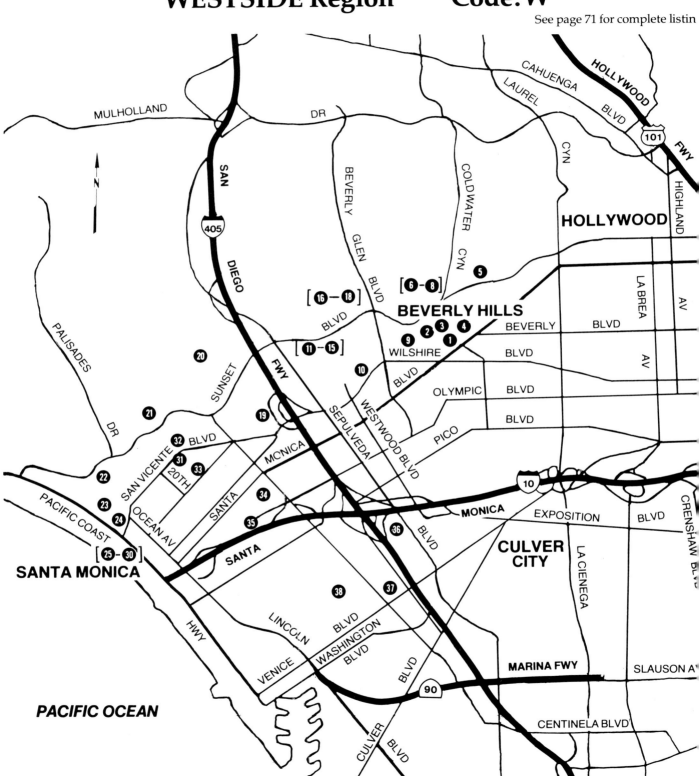

PACIFIC OCEAN

SELECTED BIBLIOGRAPHY

Bailey Hortorium. *Hortus Third*. New York: Macmillan Co., 1976.

Bean, W.J. *Trees and Shrubs Hardy in the British Isles*. London: Royal Horticultural Society, M. Bean, and John Murray, publishers, 1976.

Brandis, Dietrich. *Forest Flora of India*. London: W.H. Allen & Co., 1874.

Cribb, A.B. and J.W. Cribb. *Useful Wild Plants in Australia*. Sydney: Collins Co., 1981.

Dallimore, W. and A. Bruce Jackson. *A Handbook of Coniferae*. New York: St. Martin's Press, 1967.

Eliovson, Sima. *Flowering Shrubs, Trees, and Climbers for Southern Africa*. Cape Town: Howard Timmins, 1962.

Elliott, W. Rodger, and David L. Jones. *Encyclopedia of Australian Plants*. Melbourne: Lothian Publishing Co., 1982.

Grenier, Judson A., Doyce B. Nunis, Jr., and Jean Bruce Poole, editors. *A Guide to Historical Places in Los Angeles County*. Dubuque, Iowa: Kendall/Hunt Co., 1978.

Harris, Thistle Y. *Gardening with Australian Plants-Trees*. Melbourne: Nelson Co., 1980.

Hohn, Reinhardt, and Johannes Petumann. *Curiosities of the Plant Kingdom*. New York: Universe Books, 1980.

Holliday, Ivan and Ron Hill. *A Field Guide to Australian Trees*. Adelaide: Rigby, Ltd., 1969.

Hoyt, Roland Stewart. *Ornamental Plants for Subtropical Regions*. Anaheim, California: Livingston Press, 1978.

Kunkel, Gunther. *Flowering Trees in Subtropical Gardens*. Netherlands: The Hague, 1978.

Little, Elbert L. Jr., and Frank H. Wadsworth. *Common Trees of Puerto Rico and the Virgin Islands*. Washington, D.C.: U.S.D.A., 1964.

Menninger, Edwin A. *Flowering Trees of the World*. New York: Hearthside Press, 1962.

Menninger, Edwin A. *Fantastic Trees*. New York: The Viking Press, 1967.

Millett, Mervyn. *Australian Eucalypts*. Melbourne: Lansdowne Press, 1969.

Millett, Mervyn. *Native Trees of Australia*. Melbourne: Lansdowne Press, 1971.

Mirov, N. T. *The Genus Pinus*. New York: Ronald Press, 1967.

Moldenke, Harold, and Alma Moldenke. *Plants of the Bible*. New York: Chronica Botanica Co., 1952.

Neal, Marie C. *In Gardens of Hawaii*. Honolulu: Bernice P. Bishop Museum, 1965.

Palgrave, Keith Coates. *Trees of Southern Africa*. Cape Town: C. Struik, 1977.

Palmer, Eve and Norah Pitman. *Trees of Southern Africa*. Cape Town: A.A. Balkema Co., 1972.

Popenoe, Wilson. *Manual of Tropical and Subtropical Fruits*. New York: Hafner Press, 1948.

Riedel, Peter. *Plants for Extra-Tropical Regions*. Arcadia, California: California Arboretum Foundation, 1959.

Standley, Paul C. *Trees and Shrubs of Mexico*. Washington, D.C.: Smithsonian Institution, 1920.

Streets, R.J. *Exotic Forest Trees in the British Commonwealth*. Oxford: Clarendon Press, 1976.

Sunset Magazine. *New Western Garden Book*. Menlo Park, California: Lane Publishing, 1979.

West, Erdman, and Lillian E. Arnold. *The Native Trees of Florida*. Gainesville: University of Florida Press, 1956.

Zohary, Michael. *Plants of the Bible*. London: Cambridge University Press, 1982.

INDEX